REPOSITIONING
MARKETING IN AN ERA OF COMPETITION, CHANGE, AND CRISIS

Jack Trout
with Steve Rivkin

New York • Chicago • San Francisco • Lisbon • London
Madrid • Mexico City • Milan • New Delhi • San Juan
Seoul • Singapore • Sydney • Toronto

The *McGraw-Hill* Companies

1 2 3 4 5 6 7 8 9 0   DOC/DOC   0 1 4 3 2 1 0 9

ISBN: 978-0-07-163559-2
MHID: 0-07-163559-9

McGraw-Hill books are available at special quantity discounts to use as premiums and sales promotions, or for use in corporate training programs. To contact a representative, please visit the Contact Us pages at www.mhprofessional.com.

This book is printed on acid-free paper.

CONTENTS

PROLOGUE

This turned out to be a difficult book to write because I've already written so much on this subject. How do you not repeat yourself when you're revisiting a subject you started writing about in 1969?

You can't. So you avid readers of my work might spot some things I've mentioned in one of my 15 other books. If so, bear with me, because there is a lot of new material that better reflects what is happening in today's world.

Long ago, my ex-partner and I wrote a book entitled *Positioning: The Battle for Your Mind.* Recently, it was named one of the 100 best business books of all time. While positioning has become an important concept in business, it has a twin concept that has been quietly residing in this book while receiving little attention. The twin's name is *repositioning,* and it is time for this concept to emerge into the light of the marketplace. There are three reasons, and they all begin with the letter *c:* competition, change, and crisis.

Interestingly, in the 1980 book, repositioning could be found only in Chapter 8 as a way to hang a negative on your competitor.

I'll cover the use of competitive repositioning in a later chapter. Today, you see a lot more examples of this competitive strategy, although not as many as I would like. My recent favorite was Denny's restaurants, which hung "candy breakfast" on competitors such as IHOP while talking about its "real breakfast."

Where you see very aggressive competitive repositioning is in the world of politics. Those folks have it down to a science. Remember when the Republicans hung "flip-flop" on John Kerry? Quite unfair, but very effective. The Democrats got even in the 2006 midterm elections when they hung "incompetent" on the Republicans. When you consider the response to Katrina and our financial crisis, this turned out to be quite fair and very effective.

Repositioning to Cope with Change

Initially, repositioning's raison d'être was coping with competition. What has emerged is its use to handle the rapid technological change that is enveloping many products. Harvard professor Clayton Christensen wrote a seminal book on this subject entitled *The Innovator's*

Dilemma. In it, he coined the concept of "disruptive technologies." It described how these technologies can keep well-managed companies from staying atop their industries.

The bottom line is that in complex categories such as telephony, computers, medical devices, or film or in simple categories such as retailing, textbooks, greeting cards, or classroom instruction, change is taking its toll. In a later chapter we'll talk more about all this.

Interestingly, I've worked with a number of the companies that Christensen used as examples. My work was based on how to use repositioning to cope with this kind of change. The trick is to figure out a way to adjust your perceptions to accommodate this very threatening change.

He writes about the demise of Digital Equipment, the company that rode the minicomputer to the heights of becoming the world's second largest computer company. I was in a room with Ken Olsen, the founder of DEC, and his brother Stan Olsen. Our presentation was about a repositioning strategy to deal with the arrival of the desktop computer in business via the IBM PC, a technology that threatened the minicomputer. He chose to wait and see what IBM did and then "beat their specs." (That was like a German officer at the Normandy invasion waiting to see what the Allies did.)

I was in the room with the CEO of Xerox with a repositioning strategy presentation on how to cope with the arrival of laser printing, which threatened to undermine the traditional copying of documents. He didn't see the urgency or the need for the company to change its plans. (Hewlett-Packard went on to build an enormous business because of this decision.)

I was at Sears with a repositioning strategy on how to survive against the big-box stores that were putting it out of a business it had once dominated. Once again, management didn't choose to change its strategy and do what had to be done to survive, which is now a very questionable proposition.

The Innovator's Dilemma certainly laid out the problem. What Christensen failed to do was to outline a marketing strategy on how to deal with this problem of change. He didn't understand repositioning.

Repositioning in a Crisis

Now we are faced with the most recent *c,* or crisis. First, we have a macro crisis. Suddenly all of the world's companies have to adjust their plans to an environment that can only be described as terrifying. Once again, repositioning comes into play. In other words, how do you adjust your perceptions so as to communicate value, a concept that is on everyone's mind? You're seeing a lot of this built around price promotion. Hyundai, the Korean car company, has come up with an "if you lose your job" offer. Others just offer lower prices or buy one and get the next one free or a deep discount. I would rather see a company talk about value instead of price, which can lead to a downward spiral, as competitors also have pencils with which to mark things down.

You've probably noticed how the food brands are competing to stretch a dollar. Del Monte is promoting its canned foods as being better value than frozen. Oscar Mayer Deli Fresh meats taste "Deli fresh but without the deli counter price." You get the idea.

Then, of course, there is the micro crisis. This is where a company such as AIG or GM has to clearly reposition itself if it is to survive. This is always a tricky piece of business, as you are trying to change minds, which is never easy and sometimes impossible.

When you consider the three cs of competition, change, and crisis, you can see why repositioning is a strategy whose time has finally come. So read on.

PART 1

COMPETITION

In such things as war, the errors which proceed from a spirit of benevolence are the worst.

—Karl von Clausewitz

If there's one thing that has changed dramatically during my many years in business, it is the amazing increase in the level of competition. Now it comes at you from every part of the world and shows no signs of decreasing.

Competition isn't as difficult when markets are growing. In other words, all boats are rising. But what happens when all boats are going down? Where do you get your business? The answer is obvious: from other boats. So, in many ways, you'll have to pick up your weapons and be prepared to attack your competitors.

CHAPTER ONE

THE FOUNDATION

It's important that we review the essence of positioning, as it is also the foundation of repositioning. We have to reprise some of the prior writings on this subject. If by chance you remember verbatim what's been written, hang in there.

Positioning is how you differentiate yourself in the mind of your prospect. It's also a body of work on how the mind works in the process of communication.

Repositioning is how you adjust perceptions, whether those perceptions are about you or about your competition. (More on this in subsequent chapters.) In both cases, in order for your strategy to work, you must understand how the mind works or how people think.

So, for those of you who have missed our many books, speeches, and articles on the subject, here's a synopsis of how the mind works and the key principles of positioning.

By understanding how the mind works, you'll be prepared to better implement positioning and its twin, repositioning.

Minds Can't Cope

While the mind may still be a mystery, we know one thing about it for certain: it's under attack.

Most Western societies have become totally "overcommunicated." The explosion in media forms and the ensuing increase in the volume of communications have dramatically affected the way people either take in or ignore the information that is offered to them.

Overcommunication has changed the whole game of communicating with and influencing people. What was overload in the 1970s has turned into megaload in the new century.

Here are some statistics to dramatize the problem:

- More information has been produced in the last 30 years than in the previous 5,000.
- The total of all printed knowledge doubles every four or five years.
- One weekday edition of the *New York Times* contains more information than the average person in

seventeenth-century England was likely to come across in a lifetime.

- More than 4,000 books are published around the world every day.
- The average white-collar worker uses 70 kilograms (154 pounds) of copy paper a year—twice the amount consumed 10 years ago.

Electronic Bombardment

And what about the electronic side of our overcommunicated society?

Every day, the World Wide Web grows by a million electronic pages, according to *Scientific American*, adding to the many hundreds of millions of pages already online.

Everywhere you travel in the world, satellites are beaming endless messages to every corner of the globe. By the time a child in the United Kingdom is 18, he has been exposed to 140,000 TV commercials. In Sweden, the average consumer receives 3,000 commercial messages a day.

In terms of advertising messages, 11 countries in Europe now broadcast well over 6 million TV commercials a year. Television has exploded from a dozen channels to a thousand channels. All this means that your differentiating idea must be as simple and as visible as possible and must be delivered over and over again on all media. The politicians try to stay "on message." Marketers must stay "on differentiation."

Minds Hate Confusion

Human beings rely more heavily on learning than any other species that has ever existed.

Learning is the way in which animals and humans acquire new information. Memory is the way in which they retain that information over time. Memory is not just your ability to remember a phone number. Rather, it's a dynamic system that's used in every other facet of thought processing. We use memory to see. We use it to understand language. We use it to find our way around.

So, if memory is so important, what's the secret of being remembered?

When asked what single event was most helpful to him in developing the theory of relativity, Albert Einstein is reported to have answered: "Figuring out how to think about the problem."

Half the battle is getting to the essence of the problem. Generally speaking, this means having a deep understanding of your competitors and their place in the mind of your prospect.

It's not about what you want. It's about what your competitors will let you do.

The Power of Simplicity

The basic concept of some products predicts their failure—not because they don't work but because they don't make sense. Consider Mennen's vitamin E deodorant. That's right, you sprayed a vitamin under your arms. That doesn't make sense unless you want the healthiest, best-fed armpits in the nation. It quickly failed.

Consider the Apple Newton. It was a fax, beeper, calendar keeper, and pen-based computer. Too complex. It's gone, and the much simpler iPhone is an enormous success.

The best way to really enter minds that hate complexity and confusion is to oversimplify your message. Some of the most powerful programs are those that focus on a single word (Volvo: safety; BMW: driving). The lesson here is not to try to tell your entire story. Just focus on one powerful differentiating idea and drive it into your prospect's mind.

That sudden hunch, that creative leap of the mind that "sees" in a flash how to solve a problem in a simple way, is something quite different from general intelligence. If there's any trick to finding that simple set of words, it's being ruthless about how you edit the story you want to tell.

Anything that others could claim just as well as you can, eliminate. Anything that requires a complex analysis to prove, forget. Anything that doesn't fit with your customers' perceptions, avoid.

Minds Are Insecure

Pure logic is no guarantee of a winning argument. Minds tend to be both emotional and rational. Why do people buy what they buy? Why do people act the way they do in the marketplace?

When you ask people why they made a particular purchase, the responses they give are often not very accurate or very useful.

That may mean that they really do know, but they are reluctant to tell you the real reason. More often, however, they really don't know precisely what their own motives are.

For when it comes to recall, minds tend to remember things that no longer exist. That's why recognition of a well-established brand often stays high over a long period, even if advertising support for that brand is dropped.

In the mid-1980s, an awareness study was conducted on blenders. Consumers were asked to recall all the brand names they could. General Electric came out number two—even though GE hadn't made a blender for 20 years.

Buying What Others Buy

More often than not, people buy what they think they should have. They're sort of like sheep, following the flock.

Do most people really need a four-wheel-drive vehicle? (No.) If they do, why didn't these become popular years ago? (They weren't fashionable.)

The main reason for this kind of behavior is insecurity, a subject about which many scientists have written extensively. If you've been around a long time, people trust you more and feel secure in their purchase of your product. This is why heritage is a good differentiator.

Minds are insecure for many reasons. One reason is perceived risk in doing something as basic as making a purchase. Behavioral scientists say that there are five forms of perceived risk.

1. *Monetary risk.*
   (There's a chance that I could lose money on this.)
2. *Functional risk.*
   (Maybe it won't work, or maybe it won't do what it's supposed to do.)

3. *Physical risk.*

   (It looks a little dangerous. I could get hurt.)

4. *Social risk.*

   (I wonder what my friends will think if I buy this.)

5. *Psychological risk.*

   (I might feel guilty or irresponsible if I buy this.)

All this explains why people tend to love underdogs but buy from the perceived leaders. If everyone else is buying it, I should be buying it.

Minds Don't Change

It's futile trying to change minds in the marketplace.

- Xerox lost hundreds of millions of dollars trying to convince the market that Xerox machines that didn't make copies were worth the money. No one would buy its computers. But people still buy its copiers.
- Coca-Cola blew both prestige and money in an effort to convince the market that it had a better thing than "the real thing." No one bought New Coke. But the Classic version sells as well as ever.
- Tropicana changed its popular "straw in the orange" packaging, and the marketplace instantly declared that it wanted its orange, not something

that looked like a private-label package. The orange is back.

When the market makes up its mind about a product, there's no changing that mind.

That said, repositioning is not about changing people's minds. It's about adjusting perceptions in their minds. More on this in later chapters.

Minds Can Lose Focus

Loss of focus is really all about line extension. And no issue in marketing is so controversial.

Companies look at their brands from an economic point of view. To gain cost efficiencies and trade acceptance, they are quite willing to turn a highly focused brand, one that stands for a certain type of product or idea, into an unfocused brand that represents two or more types of products or ideas.

Look at the issue of line extension from the point of view of the mind. The more variations you attach to the brand, the more the mind loses focus. Gradually, a well-differentiated brand like Chevrolet comes to mean nothing at all.

Scott, the leading brand of toilet tissue, line extended its name into Scotties, Scottkins, and Scott Towels.

Pretty soon writing "Scott" on a shopping list meant very little, and Charmin took over the lead. Line extension is *not* a repositioning strategy, and there is more on this in Chapter 6. Some experts will tell you that it's all about building a master brand. Don't listen to them. The result is a confused brand.

SOME SURPRISING RESEARCH

Since about 70 percent of new products are launched with existing brand names, you would think these companies would have some supporting data on the pluses of line extension. The opposite is true.

The *Journal of Consumer Marketing* noted a large-scale study of 115 new-product launches across five U.S. and U.K. markets. The study compared the market share gained by products launched under established family or corporate brand names with the market share gained by products launched under new brand names.

Share was measured two years after each brand's launch. The brand extension products performed significantly less well than the products launched with new brand names.

The *Harvard Business Review* published a study on line extension. Its observations were that, among other things, line extension weakened a brand's image and disturbed trade relations.

But despite all this, the lure of brand extensions continues to haunt the marketing world. The result: brands are weakened, and category after category is threatened with creeping commoditization.

CHAPTER TWO

THE RISE OF
THE COMPETITION

Every repositioning program has to start with the competition in mind. It's not what you *want* to do; it's what your competition will *let* you do. And unless you have a wonderful new invention or you've stumbled into a monopoly, chances are that you have some killer competitors who are trying to take your business.

If you've been out of touch in recent years, just take a look at the number of choices that are out there.

An Explosion of Competition

What has changed in business in recent decades is the amazing proliferation of product choices in just about every category. It's been estimated that there are a million standard stocking units (SKUs) in the United States.

An average supermarket has 40,000 SKUs. Now for the stunner: an average family gets 80 to 85 percent of its needs from 150 SKUs. That means there's a good chance that it will ignore 39,850 items in that store.

Buying a car in the 1950s meant choosing among models from GM, Ford, Chrysler, or American Motors. Today, you have your pick of cars, still from GM, Ford, and Chrysler, but also from Acura, Aston Martin, Audi, Bentley, BMW, Honda, Hyundai, Infiniti, Isuzu, Jaguar, Jeep, Kia, Land Rover, Lexus, Maserati, Mazda, Mercedes, Mitsubishi, Nissan, Porsche, Rolls-Royce, Saab, Saturn, Subaru, Suzuki, Volkswagen, and Volvo. There were 140 motor vehicle models available in the early 1970s. There are more than 300 today.

And the choice of tires for these cars is even more vast. It used to be Goodyear, Firestone, General Tire, and Sears. Today, at just one retail outlet called The Tire Rack, you can browse the likes of Avon, B.F. Goodrich, Bridgestone, Continental, Dick Cepek, Dunlop, Firestone, Fuzion, General Tire, Goodyear, Hankook, Hoosier, Kumho, Michelin, Pirelli, Sumitomo, Uniroyal, and Yokohama.

The big difference is that what used to be national markets with local companies competing for business have become a single global market with everyone competing for everyone's business everywhere.

Competition in Health Care

Consider something as basic as health care. In the old days, you had your doctor, your hospital, Blue Cross, and perhaps Aetna/US Healthcare, Medicare, or Medicaid.

Now your hospital has to compete with freestanding clinics set up by its own doctors, not to mention other hospitals in the same town plus satellite operations from hospitals in the next county or the next state.

Even national hospital brands such as the Mayo Clinic and the Cleveland Clinic create localized competition. The Mayo Clinic, based in Minnesota, has facilities in Scottsdale, Arizona, and Jacksonville, Florida. The less well-known but equally highly rated Cleveland Clinic now has locations outside its native Ohio in Florida, in Toronto, and even in Abu Dhabi.

You want health insurance? (And who doesn't?) If you live in New Jersey, you have your choice of six large companies: Aetna, AmeriHealth, Cigna, HealthNet, Horizon BlueCross BlueShield, and Oxford. That seems like a choice any well-informed consumer could make. Oh, we should mention one thing: these six companies offer no fewer than 100 different plans. (By the time you wade through all those choices, you'll have a raging migraine!)

And stand by for the latest from Washington: the Obama administration has big plans to offer its own brand of health insurance.

It's gotten so confusing that magazines like *US News & World Report* have taken to rating hospitals and HMOs to make our choice easier. Want to know the top-rated plans as of 2009? Check out http://www .usnews.com/listings/health-plans/commercial.

The federal government and almost every state publish health-care "report cards" for the public. You'll find physicians and hospitals listed according to clinical outcome measures, as well as member satisfaction, administrative data, and professional/organizational data.

Maybe you prefer a private source for your medical information. HealthGrades.com is the leading independent health-care ratings organization. To guide you to better care providers, HealthGrades has reports and ratings on 750,000 physicians, 5,000 hospitals, and 16,000 nursing homes.

It's gotten so confusing that people aren't worrying about getting sick. They're worrying more about where to go to get better.

Competition in Consumer Electronics

Let's say you're in the market for a new CD player and recorder, speakers, and earphones. So you wander into your local Best Buy and spend some time in the audio aisle. You'll find no fewer than 21 choices: Bose, Chestnut Hill Sound, Coby, Crosley, Denon, Harman Kardon,

Insignia, ION Audio, Klipsch, Logitech, Numark, Panasonic, Philips, Pioneer, Polk Audio, Sharp, Sonos, Sony, Stanton, Technics, and Yamaha. (Do your ears hurt yet?)

Given the fact that most components can be mixed and matched, that means you have the opportunity to create more than 100,000 different audio setups. (Now we know your ears hurt.)

Competition Is Spreading

What we just described is what has happened to the U.S. market, which, of the world's markets, has by far the most choice (because our citizens have the most money and the most marketing people trying to get it from them).

Consider an emerging nation like China. After decades of buying generic food products manufactured by state-owned enterprises, China's consumers can now choose from a growing array of domestic and foreign brand-name products each time they go shopping. According to a recent survey, a national market for brand-name food products has already begun to emerge. Already China has 135 "national" food brands from which to pick.

Some markets are far from emerging. Countries like Liberia, Somalia, North Korea, and Tanzania are so poor and chaotic that choice is but a gleam in people's eyes.

The Law of Division

What drives choice is the law of division, which was described in *The 22 Immutable Laws of Marketing*.

Like an amoeba dividing in a petri dish, the marketing arena can be viewed as an ever-expanding sea of categories. A category starts off as a single entity—computers, for example. But over time, the category breaks up into other segments: mainframes, minicomputers, workstations, personal computers, laptops, notebooks, and pen computers.

Like the computer, the automobile started off as a single category. Three brands (Chevrolet, Ford, and Plymouth) dominated the market. Then the category divided. Today, we have luxury cars, moderately priced cars, and inexpensive cars; full-size, intermediate, and compacts; sports cars, hatchbacks, coupes, hybrids, diesels, four-wheel-drive vehicles, SUVs, RVs, minivans, crossovers, and suburbans (station wagons on steroids).

In the television industry, ABC, CBS, and NBC once accounted for 90 percent of the viewing audience. Now we have network, independent, cable, satellite, and public television. Today, a wired household may have 900 channels from which to choose (CNN on channel 25, the Golf Channel on 145, Encore Westerns on 353, Animal Planet HD on 757). With all that, if you flip through the channels to try to find something to watch, by the time you find it, the show will be over.

"Division" is a process that is unstoppable. If you have any doubts, consider the information on the explosion of choice in Table 2.1.

The "Choice Industry"

All this has led to the emergence of an entire industry dedicated to helping people with their choices. We've already talked about the health-care report cards.

Everywhere you turn, someone is offering advice on things like which of the 8,000 mutual funds to buy. Or how to find the right dentist in St. Louis. Or the right MBA program from among hundreds of business schools. (Which one will help me get a Wall Street job?)

The Internet is filled with dot-coms that can help you find and select anything you can imagine, all promised at rock-bottom prices.

Magazines like *Consumer Reports* and *Consumers Digest* deal with the onslaught of products and choices by rotating the categories on which they report. The only problem is that they go into so much detail that you're more confused than you were when you started.

Consumer psychologists say that this sea of choices is driving us bonkers. Consider what Carol Moog, Ph.D.,

Table 2.1 The Explosion of Competition

Item	Early 1970s	Late 1990s
Vehicle models	140	260
KFC menu items	7	14
Vehicle styles	654	1,212
Frito-Lay chip varieties	10	78
SUV styles	8	38
Breakfast cereals	160	340
PC models	0	400
Software titles	0	250,000
Soft drink brands	20	87
Bottled water brands	16	50
Milk types	4	19
Colgate toothpastes	2	17
Magazine titles	339	790
Mouthwashes	15	66
New book titles	40,530	77,446
Dental flosses	12	64
Community colleges	886	1,742
Prescription drugs	6,131	7,563
Amusement parks	362	1,174
OTC pain relievers	17	141
TV screen sizes	5	15
Levi's jean styles	41	70
Houston TV channels	5	185
Running shoe styles	5	285
Radio stations	7,038	12,458
McDonald's items	13	43
Contact lens types	1	36

has to say on the subject: "Too many choices, all of which can be fulfilled instantly, indulged immediately, keeps children—and adults—infantile. From a marketing perspective, people stop caring, get as fat and fatigued as geese destined for foie gras, and lose their decision-making capabilities. They withdraw and protect against the overstimulation; they get 'bored.'"

Choice Can Be a Turnoff

The typical argument is that extensive choice is appealing. But as Dr. Moog suggests, it can actually be a turnoff. Choice can hinder the motivation to buy.

Consider the research done on 401(k) plans and the employees who sign up for them. Researchers studied data on 800,000 employees in 647 plans in 69 industries.

What happened? As the number of fund options increased, employee participation rates dropped. Too many choices spelled confusion. And confusion led to, "No thanks."

Swarthmore College sociology professor Barry Schwartz wrote a book about these turnoffs. He called it *The Paradox of Choice*. Speaking at an industry forum in 2006, he said:

> People are so overwhelmed with choice that it tends to
> paralyze them. Too much choice makes people more likely
> to defer decisions. It raises expectations and makes people

blame themselves for choosing poorly. You don't expect much if there are only two pairs of jeans to choose from. If there are hundreds, you expect one to be perfect.*

You Have to Be Careful

If you ignore your uniqueness and try to be everything for everybody, you quickly undermine what makes you different. Consider Chevrolet. Once the dominant good-value family car, Chevrolet tried to add "expensive," "sporty," "small," and "truck" to its identity. Its "differentness" melted away, as did its business.

If you ignore changes in the market, your difference can become less important. Consider Digital Equipment Corporation (DEC). Once the premier U.S. minicomputer manufacturer, it ignored the changing technology that was making desktop computing the driving force in the office. Its "differentness" became less apparent. DEC is now deceased, having been absorbed by Compaq, which in turn was absorbed by Hewlett-Packard.

If you stay in the shadow of your larger competitors and never establish your differentness, you will always be weak. Consider Westinghouse. It never emerged from the shadow of General Electric. Today, Westinghouse is

---

* Jack Trout, *Differentiate or Die* (Hoboken, N.J.: John Wiley & Sons, Inc., 2008).

no longer with us. Or consider Goodrich. Over the years, Goodrich could reinvent the wheel and Goodyear would get all the credit for it. Because of the name confusion with its larger competitor, it was all but impossible for Goodrich to separate itself in the minds of its prospects. No one ever says, "Let's get Goodrich tires."

It's an unforgiving world out there, and things will only get worse. This is why you must learn the art of repositioning as a way to deal with your competitors.

CHAPTER THREE

REPOSITIONING
THE COMPETITION

As you read in the pro-
logue, the original concept behind repositioning was
hanging a negative on your competitor as a way to set
up a positive.

In recent times, you've been seeing more of this as
companies battle for scarce consumer dollars amid the
recession. Kodak, a film company, contrasts its ink-jet
printers with those from unnamed "big printer companies" that cost a lot of money. The positive for Kodak is
being affordable. It even sends people to a Web site to
calculate how much money they have lost by owning another brand. Apple has hung "nerdy" on PCs. Its positive is Apple's coolness. (More on this in Chapter 8.)

Similarly, McDonald's has been trying to hang the
"Snobby coffee" label on Starbucks as it goes out to
promote its lattes and cappuccinos. It even has a Web

site called Unsnobbycoffee.com where it assures customers that they will not need to learn a "second language" to order drinks.

Take Care When Attacking

Sometimes no one in a category is a winner.

John Zhang, a Wharton marketing professor, has found that combative ads—the sort of comparative spots that beer makers, particularly Anheuser-Busch and Miller, are famed for—may backfire. Instead of pulling consumers to an advertiser, they may just make people indifferent to all offerings in a product category. And that, in turn, can lead to lower profits for everyone as businesses cut prices to lure these buyers.*

When you go forth to attack your competitor, beware of getting attacked in return. Campbell's, for example, launched a campaign last year for a new line of ready-made soups. These ads asserted that a rival, Progresso, used monosodium glutamate (MSG). In the end, both brands suffered. Progresso responded with an ad saying that Campbell's also used MSG.

* knowledge.wharton.upenn.edu/article.cfm?articleid=1496; accessed June 14, 2006.

Many years ago Scope hung "bad taste" on Listerine by claiming that a user would end up with "medicine breath." That did set up the "good tasting" idea for Scope, but things did not go as planned. Listerine retaliated with the law of candor and the concept, "The taste you hate twice a day." The point it made: with a taste that bad, it must kill a lot of germs. Point and counterpoint.

Finding a Weakness

Repositioning a competitor often comes down to finding a weakness in the leader's strength and attacking at that point.

That's not a misprint. We mean "find a weakness in the leader's strength," not "find the leader's weakness." Sometimes leaders have weak points that are just weak points and not an inherent part of their strength. They may have overlooked such a point, considered it unpleasant, or forgotten about it. But there is another kind of weakness, a weakness that grows out of strength. As the Avis ads used to say, "Rent from Avis. The line at our counter is shorter." It's hard to see how Hertz could counter this repositioning strategy. This is a weakness that's inherent in Hertz's position as the largest rent-a-car company, as it is for most leaders.

The same kind of thinking can be used against any big, ubiquitous brand. How would you go against Campbell's soup, for example? Forget taste; forget price. As a matter of fact, forget everything that's inside the can and concentrate on the can itself. That's where Campbell's is vulnerable.

Cans rust. But Campbell's has hundreds of millions of dollars worth of can-making equipment that it can't walk away from very easily. However, such limitations wouldn't affect a new competitor, which could try plastic, glass, or aseptic packaging—then play "kick the can" with Campbell's.

Don't expect any company to pick up on these concepts soon. Good competitive repositioning ideas are extremely difficult to sell because they are negative in nature. They go against the "positive thinking" grain of most management people.

Russia's Mountain Water War

Sometimes a company's marketing can be a weakness. The number one mineral water in Russia is a brand called Aqua Minerale. In fact, it's a brand owned by PepsiCo, so it's not surprising that it has excellent marketing. It positioned the brand effectively by disguising its origin. It put "mineral" in the name and mountains on its label, thus making consumers believe that the water comes from a mountainous region. Smart.

The original mineral water in the Russian market was a Russian brand called Borjomi. Also not surprisingly, it has had muddled marketing. Since it was the original, Borjomi is perceived by older consumers as being the leader in mineral waters. But it has failed to capitalize on its origins while introducing confusing line extensions such as "Borjomi Light" and "Borjomi Springs." All this did was weaken the brand.

The obvious strategy is to use advertising to reposition Aqua Minerale as not being real mountain water, only make-believe mountain water. And real mountain water is the best. The concept would be to simply put the two labels side by side with the headline:

You can't spot real mountain water by the label.

Under the Aqua Minerale label, you would say, "This water is produced nowhere near the mountains." Under the Borjomi label you would print, "This water comes from the mountains, where nature produces the best water."

In judo, you're taught to use an opponent's momentum against him. This is a classic example of using a competitor's marketing against it.

An Attack Must Resonate

Anytime you hang a negative, it must quickly make sense to your prospect. Everyone knows that Listerine tastes terrible. Not everyone knows that Starbucks is "snobby." That idea doesn't resonate. And "MSG" in soup is an idea that's a little too complicated to resonate.

When Boar's Head deli products talks about its meats and cheeses as containing no artificial colors, artificial flavors, or trans fats, it repositions its competitors as not being very good. This resonates. Why? Because Boar's Head costs more and is sold in prestigious, quality-conscious delicatessens and gourmet stores—places that stake their reputation on quality.

Another way to express this concept is to ask whether the idea explodes in the mind. When you've presented your idea, your prospect should agree almost instantly, without further explanation or argument. The idea should be just too obvious to need prolonged consideration. If an idea doesn't "explode" or needs more explanation, it is not a good repositioning-the-competition idea. Mental "explosions" come with an almost instant acceptance, where the prospect agrees, no questions asked.

It's Not about Price

Trying to reposition the competition as being more expensive usually is not a very good strategy to pursue.

Price is often the enemy of differentiation. By definition, being different should be worth something. It's the reason that supports the case for paying a little more for a product or service, or at least the same amount.

But when price becomes the focus of a message or a company's marketing activities, you are beginning to undermine your chances to be perceived as being unique. What you're doing is making price the main consideration in picking you over your competition. That's not a healthy way to go.

Few companies find happiness with this approach, for the simple reason that every one of your competitors has access to a pencil. And with it, each of them can mark down its prices any time it wants to. And there goes your advantage.

As Harvard's Michael Porter says, cutting prices is usually insanity if the competition can go as low as you can.

THE CASE OF CHEAPER CARROTS

To support Porter's premise, we point you to a start-up company that came up with a unique packaging system for baby carrots. It was one that produced a decided price advantage over the two big suppliers that were already in the business.

To get on the supermarket shelves, the company entered the market not with better carrots but with a better price, repositioning its two big competitors as being expensive. Instantly the two big suppliers matched the upstart's price. This forced the new company to go lower, and the new price once again was matched by the established brands.

When a board member asked the management of this start-up to predict what would happen, the management predicted that the two big companies would not continue to reduce their prices because doing so was "irrational." They were losing money because of their older packaging technology.

The board member called us about this prediction. We advised him that the companies' action was perfectly rational. Why would the two companies that dominated the market make it easy for a new company with a manufacturing price advantage to get into the market? They were quite happy with things the way they were.

At the next board meeting, the management of the start-up company was encouraged to sell its new manufacturing system to one of the established brands. Which it did for a nice profit.

Everyone was happy, but another low-price strategy bit the dust.

David Ogilvy on Price   David Ogilvy, a legend along-side the likes of Rosser Reeves and Bill Bernbach, has some strong words to say about deals and price. They are certainly worth repeating:

> Any damn fool can put on a deal, but it takes genius, faith and perseverance to create a brand.
>
> The financial rewards do not always come in next quarter's earnings per share, but come they do. When Philip Morris bought General Foods for five billion dollars, they were buying brands.
>
> There used to be a prosperous brand of coffee called Chase & Sanborn. Then they started dealing. They became addicted to price-offs. Where is Chase & Sanborn today? Dead as a doornail.
>
> The manufacturers who dedicate their advertising to building a favorable image, the most sharply defined personality for their brand, are the ones who will get the largest share of market at the highest profit.
>
> The time has come to sound an alarm! To warn what is going to happen to brands if so much is spent on deals that there is no money left to advertise them.
>
> Deals don't build the kind of indestructible image which is the only thing that can make your brand part of the fabric of American life.*

* David Ogilvy, "Fiftieth Anniversary Luncheon Speech," Advertising Research Foundation, New York City, March 18, 1986.

The Key to Attacking Is Setting Up a Positive

What David Ogilvy was getting at was that what you need to build into a brand is a positive. The purpose of all that hanging a negative on your competitor is to set up that positive idea. Some years ago, Stolichnaya vodka hung "American made" on its U.S. competitors who were "making believe they were Russian." It was setting up "the Russian vodka" as its positive idea.

Many years ago, BMW introduced its automobile into the U.S. market by repositioning Mercedes as "the ultimate sitting machine." This was a set up for its long-term position of being "the ultimate driving machine." Repositioning Mercedes as a living room on wheels did indeed resonate with people, as at the time Mercedes was indeed manufacturing big limo-type cars. The first BMW was the 3 Series, which was a long way from today's 7 Series, which is also a "sitting machine." It's also the main reason that I'm not a fan of these big gadget-loaded BMWs. They are not driving machines; they are high-tech sitting machines. It's why you don't see many of them driving around.

A Missed Positive

Some years ago, I was down in Venezuela working with a big ketchup brand called Pampero. By the time we were called in, Del Monte and Heinz had nudged it from its number one position. Pampero was in a decline. What was needed was a differentiating idea beyond its current claims of "redder" or "better."

Why was Pampero better? What did the company do to its tomatoes? After some prodding, what emerged was the fact that Pampero removed the skin so as to enhance the flavor and color. It was something that its big competitors did not do in their manufacturing process.

Now that's an interesting idea, as many people are aware that most recipes using whole tomatoes call for removing the skin. Pampero could exploit this "without the skins" perception of quality and taste.

When we told the company that this was the best and only way to rebuild the brand's perception, Pampero became very upset. It seems that the company was in the midst of changing to a money-saving automated process that didn't remove the skins (like that used by Del Monte and Heinz). Pampero didn't want to hear about doing things the old-fashioned way.

Our recommendation was that Pampero stop the modernization plans, as "skins off" was the differentiating idea. Doing things the same way as your bigger competitors is how to get killed in the wars out there. What was called for was a major repositioning effort to hang "skins" on the competition. The positive was skinless tomatoes—a repositioning idea that never saw the light of day.

Repositioning a Competitor in Its Place

There are times, though rare, that your repositioning the competition strategy is not to hang a negative on it, but simply to put your lead competitor in its place—or, shall I say, in second place? This was the case in a project we did for the producers of Spanish olive oil.

Few people know that Spain is truly the dominant producer of olive oil. It generally produces more than half the world's olive oil. Italy, the number two producer, has only half Spain's production. In fact, Spain outproduces all other countries combined.

But there is a big problem: while Spain is the dominant leader in olive oil production, many people perceive Italy as the king. Because of that, Spain makes most of the oil, while Italian companies make most of the money with their olive oil brands. How do they do it? They buy their olive oil from Spain, put it in their cans and bottles, and ship it off as Italian olive oil. What should Spain do? That was a question we were asked by the Spanish producers. Our answer came in three steps.

Step 1 was to clearly reposition Spain as "the world's number one producer of olive oil." This little-known fact had to be put into the minds of the customers and prospects for olive oil. Spain's production credentials were an important part of the message. Outproducing all competitors combined is a great story. But Italy was already in people's minds, so a way had to be found to reposition it as a producer that used Spanish olive oil.

Step 2 dramatized this message by borrowing a historical fact. We suggested that Spain produce advertising that stated the following:

Two thousand years ago the Romans were our best customers. Today, they still are.

The point this message makes is that the Italians have always recognized good olive oil when they tasted it. Since Italy is known for its cooking, this is a very meaningful idea. But there was one other problem.

Step 3 was that of identification. If people were to look for Spanish olive oil, how were they to find it? So we developed a symbol or seal that enabled customers to identify oil from Spain. It was a simple seal that said, "100% olive oil from Spain." This seal was to be put on every can and bottle of pure Spanish olive oil.

This turned out to be the Avis number two program in reverse, as we repositioned Italy where it belonged: in second place.

Repositioning Commodities

Since we're talking about olive oil, let's look at other commodities. Even producers in the world of meats and produce have found ways to reposition themselves and thus create that unique selling proposition. Their successful strategies can be summed up in five ways.

1. *Identify.* Ordinary bananas became better bananas when a small Chiquita label was added to the fruit. Dole did the same for pineapple with the Dole label, as did the lettuce people by putting each head into a clear Foxy lettuce package. Of course, you then have to communicate why people should look for these labels.

2. *Personify.* The Green Giant character became the difference in a family of vegetables in many forms. Frank Perdue became the tough man behind the tender chicken.

3. *Create a new generic.* The cantaloupe people wanted to differentiate a special, big cantaloupe. But rather than call them just plain "big," they introduced a new category called Crenshaw melons. Tyson wanted to sell miniature chickens, which doesn't sound very appetizing. So it introduced Cornish game hens.

4. *Change the name.* Sometimes your original name doesn't sound like it would be something you would want to put in your mouth. Like a Chinese gooseberry. When the name was changed to kiwi fruit, the world suddenly had a new favorite fruit that it wanted to put in its mouth.

5. *Reposition the category.* Pork was just pig for many years. All that did was conjure up mental pictures of animals wallowing in the mud. Then the industry jumped on the chicken bandwagon and became "the other white meat." That was a very good move when red meat became a perceptual problem. (Unfortunately, that was then, but now is now. "Swine flu" has made life difficult for the pork people. That's an unforeseen marketing problem.)

China Is Learning

We were startled to note that China is quickly picking up on repositioning as a strategy. It's a story about plum juice, which isn't a juice but a kind of herbal tea. There is no proper English name for it, and it is a drink with more than a 300-year history in Beijing.

There is a big brand called Kang Shi Fu and a smaller competitor called Jiu Long Zhai. The big brand has about two-thirds of the market and costs considerably less. Jiu Long Zhai plum juice is 40 percent higher in price. It looks like a case for repositioning.

The reason that the big brand costs less is that it cuts a lot of corners in its recipe by using a lot of synthetics. (Sound familiar?) The smaller, more expensive juice is an all-natural product. So the obvious repositioning story is to hang "unnatural" on its big competitor as a setup to tell about Jiu Long Zhai's all-natural positive. Here's how the story was told, and it starts by admitting a negative, its high price, to get a positive of all natural.

> What we don't do
> > is why Jiu Long Zhai costs more.
> We do not mix with malic acid, caramel
> > and edible flavor. We keep things natural.
> Jiu Long Zhai.
> Because doing things the natural way
> > is the right way.

Uh, oh. China is pretty good at making things cheap. Wait until it gets pretty good at marketing, as it will then be a force. It looks as if the Chinese are learning fast.

PART 2

CHANGE

Nothing endures but change.

—Heraclitus, Greek philosopher, 475 B.C.

If you're not careful, nothing can kill a company more quickly than change. Like competition, it continues to accelerate, thanks in great measure to "disruptive technologies."

Even the largest companies are not protected from the ravages of change; In fact, the bigger a company is, the harder it will be for that company to survive. Go down and visit the corporate graveyard. You'll find some once very big companies that are quite dead.

CHAPTER FOUR

CHANGE HAPPENS; EVOLUTION IS REALITY

After the rise of competition in recent decades, the acceleration of change is the next big problem that has made business life more difficult. And what's driving this change is technology.

No one has presented all this better than Clayton Christensen in his book *The Innovator's Dilemma*. I would urge everyone who hasn't read it to get a copy. Even just reading the foreword is worth the money.

Christensen has coined the concept of "disruptive technology" as the enemy of established technology and the businesses it supports.

Just to give you a sense of what is driving change, Table 4.1 gives some examples borrowed from the book. It's pretty scary.

Table 4.1

Established Technology	Disruptive Technology
Silver halide photographic film	Digital photography
Wireline telephony	Mobile telephony
Circuit-switched telecommunications networks	Packet-switched communications networks
Notebook computers	Hand-held digital appliances
Desktop personal computers	Sony Playstation II, Internet appliances
Full-service stock brokerage	Online stock brokerage
New York and Nasdaq stock exchanges	Electronic communications networks (ECNs)
Full-fee underwriting of new equity and debt issues	Dutch auctions of new equity and debt issues, conducted on the Internet
Credit decisions based upon the personal judgment of bank lending officers	Automated lending decision based upon credit scoring systems
Brick-and-mortar retailing	Online retailing
Industrial materials distributors	Internet-based sites such as Chemdex and E-Steel

(continued on next page)

Table 4.1 (*continued*)

Established Technology	Disruptive Technology
Printed greeting cards	Greeting cards downloadable over the Internet
Electric utility companies	Distributed power generation (gas turbines, microturbines, fuel cells)
Graduate schools of management	Corporate universities and in-house management training programs
Classroom- and campus-based instruction	Distance education, typically enabled by the Internet
Standard textbooks	Custom-assembled, modular digital textbooks
Offset printing	Digital printing
Manned fighter and bomber aircraft	Unmanned aircraft
Microsoft Windows operating systems and applications software written in C++	Internet Protocol (IP), and Java software protocols

Table 4.1 (*continued*)

Established Technology	Disruptive Technology
Medical doctors	Nurse practitioners
General hospitals	Outpatient clinics and in-home patient care
Open surgery	Arthroscopic and endoscopic surgery
Cardiac bypass surgery	Angioplasty
Magnetic resonance imaging (MRI) and computed tomography (CT) scanning	Ultrasound—initially floor-standing machines, ultimately portable machines

Source: Clayton M. Christensen, *The Innovator's Dilemma* (Boston, Harvard Business School Press, 1997–2000).

Evolution Is Critical

Consider the carnage in the computer industry. IBM dominated the mainframe market but missed by years the emergence of minicomputers, which were technologically much simpler than mainframes. Digital Equipment Corporation created the minicomputer market and was joined by a set of other companies: Data General, Prime, Wang, Hewlett-Packard, and Nixdorf. But each of these companies, in turn, missed the desktop personal computer market. That was left to Apple,

Commodore, Tandy, and IBM's stand-alone PC division. But of all those big, once-successful companies, only three are still with us: IBM, Hewlett-Packard, and Apple. The reason: they evolved—IBM into integrated computing, Hewlett-Packard into laser printing and PCs, and Apple into the Mac, iPod, and iPhone.

Real Mail vs. E-Mail

Nothing dramatizes the problem of technological change more than the current dilemma facing Pitney Bowes, the king of the real mail market. In 1901, Arthur H. Pitney patented his first postage stamp device. Those mailing machines, which were a big deal many years ago, have been in a steady decline as the world has shifted more and more to e-mail. Why mail it when you can BlackBerry it? No handling. No stamps. Instant delivery. Now that's a disruptive technology. This sure is a case for repositioning. And what to do is obvious.

First of all, the company should recognize that the Pitney Bowes brand is riding into the sunset. How long a ride it will have is uncertain. But the money that the remaining machines earn should be invested in a new horse or brand to ride. Not feeding a brand that's been around for more than 100 years is never easy for any organization. But all that history isn't going to help. It's the Western Union problem revisited. The telephone replaced the telegraph. It was cheaper, was instantaneous, and gave you a lot more words.

Next, the company needs to build a new brand and business as the old one slowly fades away. This will not be easy, as the world is a lot more difficult than it was in 1900. Pitney Bowes has had a good run, but let's see how the next 100 years go. Since we're using a horse analogy, it's a long shot.

Silicon Graphics' Sad Saga

One of those no-longer-with-us companies is a story that we got to see up close and personal.

Back in July 1995, no computer maker was flying higher than Silicon Graphics Inc. Here's what *Business Week* had to say:

> Its dazzling three-dimensional graphics computers had a starring role animating the fearsome dinosaurs in Jurassic Park. Nintendo was using the same technology to give the Mario Brothers a face-lift and to design a new generation of arcade-like game machines. And sales were soaring. For the fiscal year ended that June 30, revenue skyrocketed 45%, to $2.2 billion—far outpacing all rivals. To top it off, CEO Edward R. McCracken was a White House regular, hobnobbing with Bill Clinton and

Al Gore. SGI's sexy image prompted a Wall Street analyst to label it "The new Apple."*

Well, all you can say now is, "It was no Apple." In April of 2009, the assets of this fallen high-tech star were sold for $25 million. A combination of mismanagement and disruptive technology did the firm in. Could it have survived? Maybe.

We got a chance to weigh in on answering this question at a time when the Windows and Intel technology (Wintel) was getting into 3D computing and offering it for a lot less than Silicon Graphics' proprietary system.

Our advice was that Silicon Graphics should not chase after Wintel, but stick to its niche of high-performance computing, where it had the credentials to support this concept. Sure, sticking to this niche meant giving up the chance at big spurts in growth. The company could reposition itself as the Porsche of computer workstations and servers. What IT person doesn't want to drive a high-performance computer? The alternative was to chase after Sun and the PC makers, which is what the company did.

My view was that it was better to be niched than to be dead. Obviously, the firm didn't take our advice.

* "The Sad Saga of Silicon Graphics," *BusinessWeek*, August 4, 1997.

Sustaining Technology

The most popular way to evolve is to use new ideas to update your brand. Finding new uses for existing products has sustained many brands.

- Scotch tape began life with a list of 300 unduplicated uses, courtesy of its manufacturer 3M. Everyday consumers dreamed up hundreds more.
- Fiberglas shows up in fishing rods, acoustic insulation, fireproofing, air filters, and textiles. (In 1941 alone, 350 patents were issued for "glass wool" products.)
- Helicopters became famous as tactical devices in warfare. Today, they herd sheep in New Zealand and shepherd the well-to-do to their getaway cottages.

Another way to keep a product relevant is to add a service. In Watsonville, California, the Granite Rock Company was selling rock and sand to local contractors. Renting trucks to move large quantities of construction material can cost a dollar or more a minute, so time was important.

What would speed things up? The company developed an automated loading system similar to a bank ATM machine. It accepted an identification card, released the materials, and printed a receipt. It called this the GraniteXpress system. Loading time used to be 24 minutes. Now customers could rock and roll in only 7 minutes.

If you value your customers' time as much as their money, you might want to look into automating a straightforward transaction. Substituting speedy machinery for clerks can make a real difference.

It can also free up your people for more scintillating work. It's no coincidence that Granite Rock has been named to *Fortune* magazine's "100 Best Places to Work" list for five consecutive years.

Evolving with a Better Name

Sometimes your name can be an anchor as you try to move forward.

Founded 50 years ago, International Service Agencies became a major player in international charitable assistance. Through workplace giving campaigns, it has provided a billion dollars in disaster relief, economic assistance, and educational aid. Its donations build homes for orphans in Africa; buy llamas in Ecuador, providing families with a source of income; and initiate weaving projects for poor women to produce hand-woven cloth for sale in their local markets.

And the organization does all this with an overhead that is dramatically below charitable industry standards.

The organization owns a dynamite domain name: www.Charity.org. But its brand name, International Service Agencies, was causing great confusion. Many potential donors believed that it was an arm of the government. It is not. Others assumed that it received federal funding. It does not.

The board of directors approved our recommendation for a new name, Global Impact, to portray the organization's mission and its work more accurately. After all, with every new project, this organization truly makes a global impact.

Evolving with a Worse Name

So your name is the SciFi Channel and you want to reposition yourself in cable TV as more than science fiction. Okay, that seems reasonable. But here's the idea that emerged: let's call ourselves the Syfy Channel.

No one who sees that in print will know what it means. (Of course, when they hear it, it will be exactly the same as it was.)

So off the company went with a big 2009 New York City launch. President David Howe announced, "The new Syfy brand embraces the new media landscape."

You just can't make up nonsense like this.

We never cease to be amazed at what can happen in the naming game. How about these current members of the "bad name hall of fame"? These are names that needed instant repositioning.

- "Lolita" beds. Woolworth stores in Britain were found to be selling beds named Lolita, designed for six-year-old girls. Angry parents put a stop to this in a hurry.
- "Incubus" sneakers. Reebok had to backpedal like crazy after it introduced a running shoe for women named Incubus. News reports promptly revealed that the dictionary definition had an unpleasant meaning: "Incubus, an evil spirit believed to descend upon and have sex with women while they sleep." That was the end of that name.

When you find yourself saddled with a stupid, damaging name, get rid of it. In 1985, Colgate-Palmolive purchased "Darkie" toothpaste, a 1920s brand with a logo of a blackface minstrel. Obviously what played in the 1920s didn't play in the 1980s. With a change of but one letter, Colgate quickly repositioned it as "Darlie," changing the logo to a man of ambiguous race with a silk top hat and tuxedo. Shrewd repositioning.

How to Evolve

The key decision you'll have to make in repositioning your product as markets evolve is to brand or not to brand. In other words, do you stay with your base brand, do you launch a subbrand, or do you start a new brand?

You've already read about Pitney Bowes and its need for a new brand. You'll read about the Lotus Development story, where the firm stayed with the Lotus brand. You'll read about how Coach leatherwear and others have launched value subbrands. You've read about Silicon Graphics, which stayed with its brand but evolved in the wrong direction. You've read about line extension, which is usually a bad thing to do.

Sometimes your decision is based on what market you want to evolve into. If you're going down-market, as you'll read about in the next segment, chances are you'll want a subbrand so as to not undermine your base brand's perceived value. If you're going upmarket, it gets a little tricky. Cadillac had little success with its $50,000 Allante because the brand had no prestige. GM, in this case, needed a new brand and a great deal of money to launch it.

Evolving distribution also can be problematic. Quick Silver is a hot surf and skateboard clothing brand. Its distribution was through small surfing retailers. Sure it could evolve to bigger retailers and sell a lot of merchandise for a while. But this is a cool youth brand, and as the company's founder said, "Big is the enemy of cool."

So as you read the next segments, keep all this in mind. If you still can't decide, call us.

Aiming Lower

Sometimes it's the clients at the other end of the food chain—those who are often overlooked by most organizations—who may be the best way to reposition your business or build a new brand.

- The check cashing industry, for example, is one of the great unknown moneymaking financial institutions in our society. Check cashers, with offices in inner cities where banks fear to tread, cash the checks of individuals who lack banking accounts. Check cashers deduct part of the check—a healthy part—as a fee, and their clients get the rest of the cash. In dealing with the lower part of the financial services market, check cashers have expanded their offerings to include electronic bill paying, lending, and a host of additional—and profitable—services.
- Retailers, too, have begun to dip their toes in the waters of the less affluent. The Yamada Group, an unconventional department store and supermarket chain in Brazil, offers its credit card to poor Brazilians who toil in the Amazon's vast off-the-books economy. Yamada cards are good only in

Yamada stores, which is just dandy with the fishermen, coconut vendors, gold miners, and street hawkers who make up its customer base. And the business is equally fine with Yamada, which reports lower-than-normal delinquency rates and higher-than-normal profitability. According to the chain's managing director, Yamada's poor clients are so appreciative of their credit cards that they pay promptly.

Aiming Higher

Ireland's C&C Group successfully repositioned its cider drink Magners Original as a premium drink in the British market.

"Cider's a cool brew now, but it wasn't always thus," C&C's chief executive told *Time* magazine. "It was thought of as a product consumed by vagrants on park benches."[*]

The cider was commonly sold in large plastic bottles at discount prices, bolstering its cheap image. Struggling with stagnant sales in the 1990s, C&C decided that the dowdy cider needed a makeover. The key ideas in its repositioning:

---

* Thomas Grose, "How Do You like Them Apples?" *Time*, May 17, 2007.

- Cut the alcohol content to 4.5 percent (about the same as most beers).
- Intensify the apple flavor.
- Stop making it available on tap in pubs and bars.
- Junk the plastic jugs and use fancy pint bottles.
- Jack up the price.
- Most important, market the reformulated drink as intended to be poured over ice, whereas traditional ciders are served at room temperature.

Putting the cider in bottles was a smart move, not only because C&C could charge more, but also because consumers could now hold the Magners brand in their hands. (It's much harder to build a brand with a draft-only product.)

The idea of serving cider over ice came from its Irish heritage. It was based on the simple fact that there wasn't great refrigeration in many Irish pubs, so consumers naturally poured it over ice.

A blurb on the new bottle urges pubkeepers and consumers to pour the cider over ice. Within a year, the Magners brand increased its sales by 260 percent.

Evolving Your Distribution

As already stated, this can be tricky, but you can find new ways to distribute as long as you don't upset your existing distribution arrangements or your image. Here are some examples:

- In 2009, a private equity firm bought the bankrupt Linens N' Things business and transformed it into an Internet-only operation. It still offers 200,000 products for the home, but now its overhead costs are lower as it competes with brick-and-mortar players like Bed Bath & Beyond.

- Nuprin was an also-ran brand of ibuprofen until it went the private-label route. The name was sold to the CVS pharmacy chain, which is now its exclusive retailer.

- Tupperware was a party-only player for decades. But now that more and more households have two adults working outside the home, Tupperware has to party a little harder. Its storage containers are now available in Target stores.

- Ditto for Avon cosmetics, which is now calling on customers in department stores.

- Even the venerable Fred Rogers, creator of the kids' TV show *Mister Rogers' Neighborhood,* found a new way to distribute his gentle message. He introduced an interactive program on the PBS Web site and a series of children's stories for www.mister rogers.org. Hey, it's a beautiful day in the cyberhood.

What's the point? There can always be another way to physically distribute whatever you're selling. Direct mail, online, kiosks in malls, kiosks in airports, door to door—think about what else you could use.

Convergence as Evolution

Over the years, we've badmouthed "convergence" as a way to evolve a product.

Creating products that do more than one thing requires sacrifice of a different kind. Designing multifunctional products forces your designers to give up what could be an outstanding single-function design for a lesser design that accommodates the extra functions.

Can a great car be a great boat at the same time? Of course not. If you want a really fast car, get a Ferrari. A fast boat? Get a Cigarette boat.

Can a great Formula One racing tire be a great passenger car tire at the same time? Of course not. (Racing tires don't have any tread.)

People want the best of the breed, not a mutt that contains several breeds.

People don't want to give up important features so that they can do other things with the product. Just because you can build it is no insurance that people will buy it.

If your difference is that your product can do a lot of things not very well, as opposed to a product that does one thing exceptionally well, you haven't got much of a difference.

Convergence to Something Else

The only time that convergence, or creating products that do more things, can work is when the product becomes something new. Consider the cell phone. Thanks to iPhones, BlackBerries, and other such devices, the cell phone is evolving beyond just making phone calls. Now you can go online, play games, find directions, take pictures, and use many other applications. The cell phone isn't really a cell phone anymore. It's become a pocket computer that does many things. That's why people stare at it more than they talk into it. That thing in your hand has become a computer screen that you can talk into, listen to, or just read if you want.

We're fast approaching a time when no one will be looking where they are going or looking at the person they are with. We'll have a rude world of people looking at their little computers. The worst will be the next generation of kids.

Evolution Failure and Success

There are reasons that companies do well at evolution. Richard Foster, a director at McKinsey & Company, laid out the reasons for failure very succinctly when he was quoted in an article in *California Management Review*:

> Of the 10 leaders in vacuum tubes in 1955 only two were left in 1975. There were three variants of error in these case histories. First is the decision not to invest in the new technology. The second is to invest but picking the wrong technology. The third variant is cultural. Companies failed because of their inability to play two games at once: To be both effective defenders of what quickly became old technologies and effective attackers with new technologies.*

Foster suggests that firms like Intel and Motorola were not saddled with internal conflict and inertia and, as they grew, they were able to recreate themselves. Other firms, like RCA, were unable to manage these multiple technological approaches; they were trapped by their successful pasts.

In contrast to RCA, consider Seiko's watch business. Seiko was the dominant Japanese watch producer in the 1960s, but Japanese firms were small players in the global watch market. Seiko's senior management team

* M. L. Tushman and C. A. O'Reilly III, "Ambidextrous Organizations: Managing Evolutionary and Revolutionary Change," *California Management Review* 38, no. 4 (1996), pp. 8–30.

made a bold bet. The company aspired to be a global leader in the business, and it experimented with alternative oscillation technologies (quartz, mechanical, and tuning fork). This pushed Seiko's transformation from merely a mechanical watchmaker into a quartz and mechanical watch company.

This move into low-cost, high-quality watches triggered wholesale change within Seiko and, in turn, within the worldwide watch industry. Even though the Swiss had invented both the quartz and tuning fork movements, they chose to reinvest in mechanical movements. But ultimately the quartz movement won the oscillation battle to become the industry standard. As Seiko and other Japanese firms prospered, the Swiss watch industry suffered.

The Problem of Inside Thinking

Enterprises that sustain their growth over a period of time are seen as successful. With that success, a "we know best" culture often develops. And why not? After all, the evidence seems to suggest that these managers and employees *do* know best.

Over time, pride can lead to overconfidence or arrogance. When people think that they have the answers and others don't, they tend not to pay much attention to those others—especially outsiders—because it seems like a waste of time.

What's the downside? An organization that is inwardly focused inevitably misses new opportunities, overlooks threats from competitors, and misreads changing customer needs. When you don't see opportunities or hazards, your sense of urgency drops. With less urgency, you are even less inclined to look outside for the new possibilities and problems. Complacency grows.

Examples abound of how success creates size, market power, and an entitlement culture, all of which, in turn, create an inward focus, a lack of understanding of external reality, and a total lack of urgency to correct the problem.

Success in repositioning must come from outside thinking. That's where the market is located.

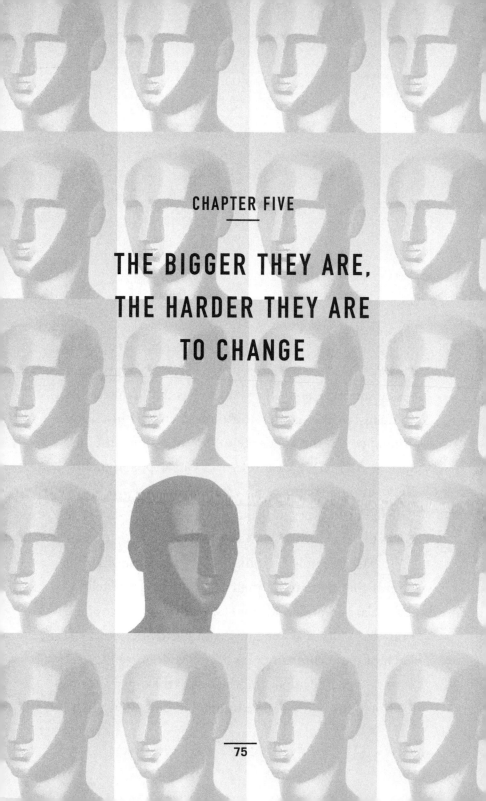

CHAPTER FIVE

THE BIGGER THEY ARE, THE HARDER THEY ARE TO CHANGE

Big is the enemy of change.

With size comes a large degree of inflexibility, ego, vested interests, and other bad things that hamstring a company in this age of the unpredictable. Just look around you at the wreckage of our largest institutions, such as AIG, GM, Merrill Lynch, Citicorp, and others. Repositioning requires a certain degree of flexibility that size makes very difficult, if not impossible. If you're going to get big, do it the way United Technologies does it. It has assembled a number of highly specialized brands that operate on their own, such as Otis elevators, Carrier air conditioners, Sikorsky helicopters, Pratt & Whitney jet engines, and Norden electronics. Each of these companies could reposition itself if necessary, with little impact on the rest of the organization. Do you think many people know that Otis is owned by

United Technologies? Does it matter? Each brand has retained the flexibility to deal with whatever happens in this fast-changing world.

When you start to study the subject of getting big, you quickly come up with a stunning amount of research and analysis that seriously questions whether bigger is better. By the time we finished, we began to wonder what in the world these CEOs were thinking about as they got trapped in the land of merger mania.

Let's start with the academics.

The Bigness Complex

Two economists produced a 400-page analysis that confronts the quintessential myth of corporate culture: that industrial giants are the handmaidens of economic efficiency. In a book entitled *Bigness Complex* (Pantheon Books, 1986), Walter Adams and James Brock argue that the preoccupation with bigness is at the heart of the United States' economic decline.

A little hindsight shows that they miscalled our "economic decline." Quite the opposite occurred: we roared off into an amazing economic expansion. They also missed the fact that these big companies have been falling apart on their own, so we don't need any government policy to keep bad bigness things from happening. And they missed the small-company explosion in high-tech land that helped propel our expansion. This only proves that you can't predict the future. But they did make some powerful points about "big."

Big Isn't More Efficient

After an extensive amount of original and observed research, the authors concluded that conglomerate bigness seldom enhances, and more typically undermines, efficiency in production.

Their key findings were

1. Optimum plant sizes tend to be quite small relative to the national market.
2. Loss of production efficiency is surprisingly small in plants that are much smaller than those of optimal scale.
3. Substantial deconcentration could be effected with only a slight sacrifice of economies of scale.

It's no wonder that big business has been replacing huge manufacturing complexes with new, smaller plants. Companies have discovered that their people can't manage their way out of the problems created by size and complexity.

Big Is Less Profitable

Richard Rumelt, a professor at the Anderson School of Management at the University of California, has some interesting insights about bigness. Here are some excerpts from an interview in the *McKinsey Quarterly*.

The Quarterly: Shifting gears a bit, Richard, can you tell us about your research on diversification and focus?

Richard Rumelt: Well, my first research on corporate strategy showed that somewhat diversified but relatively focused companies tend to outperform highly diversified companies. And that finding has held up fairly consistently over the decades. Financial theory would say that companies diversify to reduce risk, but in the business world diversification is done not to hedge risk but to sustain top-line growth. The riskiest companies—the start-ups and early-stage companies—are intensely focused. Companies begin thinking about diversification only when their growth has plateaued and opportunities for expansion in the original business have been depleted. Suddenly, they have more cash flow than they know what to do with.

The Quarterly: Why are the highly diversified companies less profitable?

Richard Rumelt: It seem that the more complex an organization gets, the more likely it is that inefficient and unproductive businesses accumulate in the nooks and crannies and back alleys—and sometimes right up there in center aisle. These businesses are subsidized by their cousin, brother, and sister businesses that are doing well, and they stick around for too long because there's a bias against shutting things down. Often we'll find that these are pet projects of senior management and cutting them would cause a huge ego blow. It's extremely unrewarding to a person's career to weed the garden inside a company. It is much easier and more popular politically to grow the company than it is to go around and disrupt everybody's neighborhood.*

Big Doesn't Attack Itself

When a company is rich and successful, it doesn't want anything to change. IBM didn't want to see its mainframe world shift to small computers. General Motors didn't want to see its big-car world shift to small cars.

As a result, inventions that undercut such a company's main business are frowned on. Rare is the big successful company that says, "Hey, that's a better idea. Let's dump our original idea." Instead, these companies

* http://www.mckinseyquarterly.com/Strategys_strategist_An_interview _with_Richard_Rumelt_2039.

quickly point out the flaws in this new idea. What they never take into consideration is the possibility that this new thing can be improved to a point where it can become what is called a disruptive technology, or one that shifts the balance of power.

Xerox invented laser printing, but it restricted this technology to its big machines so as to not affect the copier business. Hewlett-Packard ran away with the laser printing business. Kodak invented digital photography, but the company never pursued it aggressively so as to not affect the film business. A lot of people ran away with the digital photography business.

Market leaders have to be willing to attack themselves with a better idea. If they don't reposition themselves, someone else will do it by hanging a negative on them.

Big Doesn't Organize Well

Economists do touch on the difficulties of organizing big companies, but to me, the best analysis of managing size came from a British anthropologist named Robin Dunbar. In an excellent book entitled *The Tipping Point* (Little, Brown & Co., 2000), Malcolm Gladwell introduces us to Dunbar, whose work revolved around what he called social capacity, or how big a group we can run with and feel comfortable. His observation is that humans socialize in the largest group of primates because we are the only animals with brains large enough to handle the complexities of that social arrangement. His observation was that the figure of 150 seems to represent the maximum number of individuals with whom we can have a genuine social relationship that goes with knowing who they are and how they relate to us.

Gladwell extracted from Dunbar's work the following observation that gets to the heart of being too big:

> At a bigger size you have to impose complicated hierarchies and rules and regulations and formal measures to try to command loyalty and cohesion. But below 150, Dunbar argues, it is possible to achieve these same goals informally: "At this size orders can be implemented and unruly behavior controlled on the basis of personal loyalties and direct man-to-man contacts with larger groups. This becomes impossible."*

Personal Agenda

What Dunbar never envisioned was what happens in big companies. What advanced primates all have is called a reflex personal agenda. It goes like this: when faced with

* www.lifewithalacrity.com/2004/03/the_dunbar_numb.html.

a decision that could be best for the company versus one that could be best for the individual, a large percentage of the time a human primate will opt for the decision that betters his career. Another expression of this is "making your mark."

In all my years in the business, I've never seen a marketing person come into a new assignment, look around, and say, "Things look pretty good. Let's not touch a thing." On the contrary, all red-blooded marketing people want to get in there and start improving things. They want to make their mark. Just sitting there wouldn't feel right. When a company has offices full of people, you've got to expect endless tinkering with a brand. It's how people keep from getting bored.

It's also how brands get in trouble. The more people you have, the more difficult it is to manage them.

The Ultimate Tinker

Nothing dramatizes this more than the recent goings-on at Pepsi's North American beverage business.

Massimo d'Amore rode into Pepsi several years ago. Rather than just fiddling at the margins, he decided on drastic change. He wanted hipper marketing, which meant not only new ads and slogans for seven brands, but also a redesign of 1,121 bottles, cans, and packages. And he wanted it done in just seven months.

Three results are worth mentioning. The design firm in charge of all this redid the Tropicana orange juice package and eliminated one of the best brand graphic elements of all time: the straw in the orange, which visually said pure orange juice. Once it was removed, people thought they were seeing a private-brand orange juice, not Tropicana. The market rebelled, as it had done when Coke introduced New Coke. Pepsi was forced to bring back the original package design. Millions down the rathole.

Then there was a redesign of the Pepsi bottle. A perfectly good design with the Pepsi name and logo was changed by rotating the logo a few degrees and making the Pepsi name dramatically less readable. The average consumer would hardly notice this difference, which cost Pepsi millions of dollars in design fees and packaging costs.

Finally, the tinkerers mucked up its once-hot Gatorade brand. They replaced the Gatorade name on its label with a big letter "G" and shrank its signature lightning bolt. All this did was confuse consumers and shrink the brand's market share of the sports-drink market by 4.5 percent. No one will ever ask for a bottle of "G."

Will any of this improve Pepsi's long-term business? Not likely. Will the design firm that cooked all this up get more Pepsi business? Not likely.

One can only say that the personal agenda is a problem in big companies that makes things hard to manage.

Why Things Go Wrong

Studies have shown that a large percentage of mergers underperform their grand predictions of success. Two large companies that join together spend so much time on operational integration that they end up running on the fumes of their past glory and brand names. What you rarely see are new ideas or innovation. What's behind the merger of Mobil and Exxon? As best I can figure out, it's a bunch of accountants and efficiency experts figuring out how to cut costs, gain market share, and boost the stock price.

Immense resources and big brand names rarely guarantee innovation. More often, all that tradition and bureaucracy get in the way of any repositioning thinking.

The Problems Multiply

Other things that come with a big merger are double or triple the number of employees, products, shareholders, and customers. Managing all this becomes exceptionally difficult. Pretty soon, there are endless meetings about logos, cutting head counts, closing offices, selling off businesses, and figuring out how to put the right spin on all this to customers and employees.

Next, there are the problems with keeping the company's best people from taking their egos elsewhere. Pecking orders get disrupted. Everyone's trying to figure out who is up, who is down, and who is out.

The actual business at hand is buried in a flurry of rumors and time spent looking for a new job.

But what tops all the problems is what they call culture clash, or bringing together two highly complex, large, and not necessarily like-minded companies. Culture is "the way we do things around here." This includes participation in decision making, performance rewards, risk tolerance, and quality and cost orientation. All this leads to, at great expense, a great deal of touchy-feely communication and integration seminars. Team building and sensitivity training become the rage, and change management consultants ride into town.

That's what happens in U.S. mergers. When you have global mergers such as DaimlerChrysler, all that New Age stuff goes out the window. Could a German carmaker ever integrate with a Detroit carmaker? Not likely. You know what those Mercedes engineers thought of those Chrysler engineers? Not much. There's no chance that management consultants could change those attitudes. It's no wonder the marriage blew apart in short order.

Stall Points

If all that history and analysis wasn't enough to throw cold water on getting big, we came across a Washington, D.C., organization called the Corporate Strategy Board. This organization, in association with, of all corporations, Hewlett-Packard, developed a study on the theoretical limits to growth. It studied corporate "stall experiences" over four decades and concluded that big is indeed very difficult to manage for growth.

The numbers are hard to argue with. A $40 million company needs only $8 million to grow 20 percent. A $4 billion company needs $800 million. Very few new markets are that large. This means that the larger and more successful a company is, the more difficult it will become for it to maintain that pace.

Interestingly, 83 percent of the root causes of company stall points were controllable. Either strategic factors or organizational factors led to trouble. Translation: it's easy to make management mistakes with giant corporations—the bigger they are, the harder they are to manage. (Look out below!)

Bigness Gone Bad

There is no sadder story than that of AIG. Before the great crash, it was a holding company for a network of subsidiaries engaged in insurance and insurance-related activities, including property, casualty, life, financial services, retirement savings products, asset management, and aircraft leasing. It was the largest insurance company in the world. It was unmanageable.

It's no wonder that a 300-employee group in London that was insuring toxic credit default swaps took the company over the cliff. A sad, sad story that didn't have to end that way.

Many years ago, we worked for AIG doing some strategy for one of its "hobby" acquisitions, the Stowe ski area in Vermont. (CEO Hank Greenberg was a big skier.)

It became apparent that AIG's real need was to clearly reposition itself as more than just a big general and life insurance company. The obvious idea that we presented was simple but powerful: *America's answer to Lloyd's of London.*

AIG had a strong global presence in this kind of insurance, and, thanks to Hank, it was a far better managed operation than Lloyd's. But it didn't want to hear about this strategy. AIG wanted to get into financial services and everything else. It wanted to be everything for everybody. Well, we know how that worked out.

Here's a case where a company chased "change" to a place where it never should have gone. It should have stayed where it was. But more on that in the next chapter.

A CEO Wakes Up

It's fitting that I end this chapter with a positive big-company change story. It's also fitting that it be about PepsiCo, a company that I panned earlier in the chapter. In the late 1960s and early 1970s, PepsiCo was sold a bill of goods on the idea that it could reduce its income tax bills if it invested some of its huge cash flow from the soft drink and snack business into leasing companies, where the depreciation created by leasing large assets would create taxable losses for the corporation. It's the kind of thinking that big companies get talked into.

PepsiCo purchased several leasing companies, including Chandler Leasing of Waltham, Massachusetts. Chandler specialized in leasing computer equipment, but it was given the go-ahead to lease other types of assets. Because the president of Chandler liked airplanes, the company created an aircraft leasing division. Flush with Pepsi cash and huge lines of credit from Pepsi's banks, it began to lease first small aircraft, then corporate planes, and then jumbo jets.

Don Kendall, CEO of PepsiCo, came around for an annual review. My inside source reported that he was half asleep during the opening segment until the presentation showed the figures on how many aircraft the company owned and the millions of dollars of debt owed to the banks.

Suddenly, Mr. Kendall's eyes popped wide open as he watched the amount of aircraft assets threaten to pass the amount of soft drink assets in another few years. But worst of all, the company could be on the hook for an enormous amount of money if things went bad. (Sounds like AIG.) That amount of debt could sink the company.

It was probably at that moment that the CEO decided to change his corporate strategy and rid the company of aircraft leasing. It was back to soft drinks and snacks.

Nicely done, Mr. Kendall.

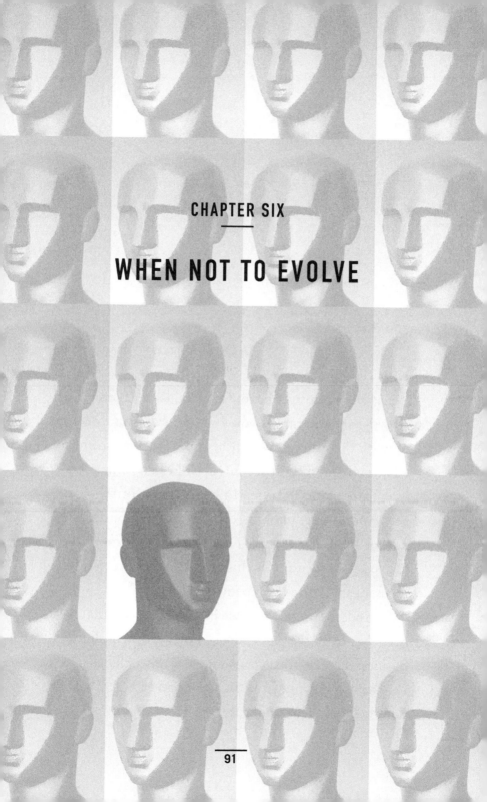

CHAPTER SIX

WHEN NOT TO EVOLVE

Should every brand and every company evolve?

The simple answer is no. Growth just for the sake of growth can be a trap, as you'll see. Evolving just to keep up with the other guys can be a mistake. (Remember what your mom said when you told her, "But everybody is doing it.") Trying to be the latest or the next-generation something can kill your existing business.

And about the worst thing you can do to yourself is fuzz up your identity, as this opens the door for a well-focused, specialized competitor.

Consider White Castle, the hamburger place that has been basically the same since the 1920s. The burger business has exploded around it, with other chains hurling themselves into grilled chicken and loaded baked potatoes and yogurt parfaits.

White Castle never changed its buildings and made only minor additions to its burgers-and-fries menu. Result: next to McDonald's, White Castle has the highest sales per unit in the category. Its ace in the hole? It is privately owned and doesn't have to answer to Wall Street, a group that is nothing but trouble.

The Growth Trap

Those friendly folks from Wall Street often create an environment that encourages bad, sometimes irrevocable things to happen. In a way, they set up a greenhouse for trouble, and as with a greenhouse, what it's all about is encouraging things to "grow." But this growth is not evolution to cope with change. It's more about the stock price.

The well-known economist Milton Friedman put it perfectly when he said, "We don't have a desperate need to grow. We have a desperate desire to grow."

That desire for growth is at the heart of what can go wrong for many companies. Growth is the by-product of doing things right. But in itself, it is not a worthy goal. In fact, growth is the culprit behind impossible goals.

CEOs pursue growth to ensure their tenures and to increase their take-home pay. Wall Street brokers pursue growth to ensure their reputations and to increase their take-home pay.

But is it all necessary? Not really. When you consider that people do damaging things to force unnecessary growth, you can say that it's a crime against the brand. This story illustrates how the desire for growth is at the root of evil doings.

We were brought in to evaluate the business plans for a large multibrand drug company. In turn, the brand managers stood up and presented their next year's plans. In the course of a presentation, a young executive warned of aggressive new competition in his category that would definitely change the balance of power. But when it came to a sales projection, he predicted a 15 percent increase. Instantly, we questioned how this could be, given the new competition.

His answer was that his group was going to do some short-term maneuvering and line extension. Long term, wouldn't this hurt the brand? Well, yes. Then why do it? Because his boss had made him put in the increase, and I would have to talk with him.

One week later, his boss admitted the problem but said that *his* boss needed the increase because of, you guessed it, Wall Street.

The 15 Percent Delusion

Carol Loomis, a well-known *Fortune* editor, wrote a landmark article on this subject that challenged the "brash predictions about earning growth that often lead to missed targets, battered stock and creative accounting." The article asked: Why can't CEOs kick the habit?

In the article, Carol laid out what has become accepted executive behavior:

> Of all the goals articulated, the most common one among good-sized companies is annual growth in earnings per share of 15 percent—the equivalent, you might say, of making the all star team. With 15 percent growth, a company will roughly double its earnings in five years. It will almost inevitably star in the stock market, and its CEO will be given, so to speak, ticker-tape parades.*

You don't have to be a rocket scientist to figure out why this happens. It's these kinds of predictions that get Wall Street's attention. It's like a love dance between Wall Street and management as they whisper sweet nothings to each other. Management wants the top analysts to follow the company and recommend its stock. Wall Street wants a winner to make analysts look good and attract more money.

But there is no reality in all this. It's all delusion.

* Carol J. Loomis, Reporter Assoc., *Fortune*, February 5, 2001.

The Real Numbers

As Loomis points out in her article, extensive research shows that few companies are able to grow 15 percent or more a year. Over the past 40 years, *Fortune* looked at 150 companies over three basic time periods (1960–1980, 1970–1990, and 1989–1999).

In each of those time frames, only three or four companies achieved the 15 percent or more earnings growth factor. About 20 to 30 companies ran at a 10 to 15 percent clip, 40 to 60 companies ran at 5 to 10 percent, 20 to 30 at 0 to 5 percent, and 20 to 30 actually ran at a negative number. That's right, there were as many big losers as big winners.

Overall, during that 40-year period, the after-tax profits grew at an annual rate of just over 8 percent. This means that any company doing 15 percent was running at almost twice the rate of the general population of companies.

With that reality, it's not surprising that companies start to do some bad things to keep their growth rate up.

Insidious Stock Options

Where Wall Street often sneaks into the equation is in the form of stock options. When managers or even middle-level employees are looking at their stock options, they start to get concerned about that next quarter. They want to make sure that their options stay healthy, so they are quick to cut corners or not make a long-term decision that is good for the business but could take several cents off earnings. They read the papers. You miss your earnings estimate by a few pennies and Wall Street will take your stock down 20 percent. That could put those options underwater and create an army of employees with very long faces.

A client of mine who is in the pizza business reported just such an example of short-term versus long-term thinking. One of his people had come across a new flour-milling system that dramatically improved the dough-making process. The people in charge hung back from quickly spending the money on what the owner thought was the right thing to do. The reason for the delay was that the costs would affect quarterly earnings estimates. As he put it, "My people were robbing from Peter (quality improvement) to pay Paul (Wall Street)."

Needless to say, he's trying to get away from the options method of paying his people.

Ego Problems

Another thing that happens to CEOs when they miss their brave but unrealistic goals is that their ego takes a hit at the same time that their stock takes a hit. With all the financial news reporting out there, Wall Street's devaluing of a stock puts the CEO in the glaring light of bad publicity. Suddenly, everyone is writing stories about this CEO and how he missed his numbers.

One day Carly Fiorina was a hero at Hewlett-Packard. The next day, people were writing about her overambitious targets and how she was losing her credibility with Wall Street. If you're thick of skin, it's no big deal. But guess who reads those same articles? The board of directors and your employees. Taking a public hit like that erodes your reputation and wears on you. It makes you cautious, which isn't always such a good thing. (We know what happened to Carly.) Think how a general would feel if he started getting negative press right in the middle of a campaign. It certainly wouldn't encourage much more boldness on his part. That, in turn, could turn out to be a big plus for the enemy.

But enough about Wall Street.

The "Latest" Trap

One of the better evolution strategies is to come up with the latest or next generation of product in a category.

The iPod's digital music strategy wiped out the Walkman, much to Sony's embarrassment. It was truly the next generation of portable music.

But the latest doesn't always work, and there are some pitfalls in the next-generation game that you must avoid at all costs. If you don't, you could have real problems. Here's an outline of what to avoid.

- *Don't solve a nonexistent problem.* Your next-generation product must solve a real problem, not one that's unimportant. Dow Chemical introduced Dowtherm 209, a new antifreeze coolant that was billed as "doing no harm if it leaked into the crankcase." (By the way, it cost twice as much as old-generation coolants.) The trouble was that conventional coolants hardly ever leaked into the engine. Why pay twice as much to solve a nonexistent problem? Most people didn't.

- *Don't mess with tradition.* There are real problems that people don't want solved. They like the old-fashioned way. Nothing is as traditional as eating unshelled peanuts at the ballpark. Unfortunately, everyone is up to his ankles in shells by the end of the game. To avoid the shell mess, Harry M. Stevens introduced preshelled peanuts in cellophane packages. People were outraged. Sales fell; complaints rose. Back to walking on shells.

- *It must be better.* Why go for the next thing if it isn't a better thing? The U.S. mint brought out the

Susan B. Anthony $1 coin as a replacement for the $1 bill. To the mint, it was a big improvement because it would save $50 million a year in printing and processing costs. To the public, there were no perceived benefits. It looked like a quarter, and many thought it was ugly. Good-bye, Suzy.

Minds Can Lose Focus

Evolving a brand is a tricky piece of work because you can fuzz up your identity. Let's continue the discussion that we started in Chapter 1.

In days gone by, most big brands were clearly perceived by their customers. The mind, like a camera, had a very clear picture of what its favorite brands were all about.

When Anheuser-Busch proudly proclaimed, "This Bud's for you!" the customer knew exactly what was being served.

The same went for Miller High Life, or plain old Coors Beer.

But in the past decade, Budweiser has flooded the market with regulars, lights, drafts, clears, cold-brewed, dry-brewed, and ice-brewed beers.

Now the statement "This Bud's for you" can elicit only the question, "Which one do you have in mind?"

That once-clear perception in the mind is now badly out of focus. It's no wonder that the King of Beers is starting to lose its following.

A Matter of Perspective

The difference in views on this subject is essentially a perspective. Companies look at their brands from an economic point of view. To gain cost efficiencies and trade acceptance, they are quite willing to turn a highly focused brand, one that stands for a certain type of product or idea, into an unfocused brand that represents two or three or more types of products or ideas.

We look at the issue of line extension from the point of view of the mind. The more variations you attach to the brand, the more the mind loses focus. Gradually, a brand like Chevrolet comes to mean nothing at all.

Scott, the leading brand of toilet tissue, line-extended its name into Scotties, Scottkins, and Scott Towels. Pretty soon "Scott" flunked the shopping-list test. (You can't write down "Scott" and have it mean anything.)

Danger: A Well-Focused Specialist

Things would have been fine in the land of Scott if the likes of Mr. Whipple and his squeezable Charmin tissue hadn't arrived on the scene. (The more you lose focus, the more vulnerable you become.) It didn't take long for Charmin to become the number one tissue.

The course of business history seems to verify our concerns.

For years, Procter & Gamble's Crisco brand was the leading shortening. Then the world turned to vegetable oil. Of course, Procter & Gamble developed Crisco Oil.

So who's the big winner in the corn-oil melée? That's right, Mazola.

The next move was to no-cholesterol corn-oil margarine. So Mazola introduced Mazola Corn Oil Margarine.

So who's the winner in the corn-oil-margarine category? You're right; it's Fleischmann's.

In each case, the specialist or the well-focused competitor was the winner.

The Specialist's Weapons   Here are some thoughts on why the specialist brand appears to make such an impression on the mind.

First, the specialist can focus on one product, one benefit, and one message. This focus enables the marketer to put a sharp point on the message that quickly drives it into the mind. For example, Domino's Pizza can focus on its home delivery. Pizza Hut has to talk about both home delivery and sit-down service.

Duracell can focus on long-lasting alkaline batteries. Eveready had to talk about flashlight, heavy-duty, rechargeable, and alkaline batteries. (Then the company got smart and went to the Energizer only, a good move on Eveready's part.)

Castrol can focus on its oil for high-performance small engines. Pennzoil and Quaker State are marketed for all types of engines.

Another weapon of the specialist is the ability to be perceived as the expert or the best. Philadelphia is the best cream cheese (the original, so to speak). Titleist is the best golf ball.

Finally, the specialist can become the "generic" for the category. Xerox became the generic word for copying ("Please Xerox that for me").

Federal Express became the generic word for overnight delivery ("I'll FedEx it to you").

3M's Scotch tape became the generic word for cellophane tape ("I'll Scotch-tape it together").

Even though the lawyers hate it, making the brand name a generic is the ultimate weapon in the marketing wars. But it's something that only a specialist can do. The generalist can't become a generic.

Nobody ever says, "Get me a beer from the G.E."

Some companies see evolution through a lens of what others are doing. This can be a problem.

The "Everyone Is Doing It" Trap

Hearst Magazines is another privately held company that is doing very well at a time when its magazine competitors are doing very badly. Its success is based on not doing what everyone else is doing.

In 2008, its new *Food Network* magazine had a paid circulation of 300,000. By the end of 2009, the circulation will rise above 1.1 million.

As reported in the *New York Times*, Hearst Magazines, a unit of the Hearst Corporation, has repeatedly gone against the grain, from its traditional tight cost control in an often profligate business, to lagging years behind in building magazine Web sites, to recently raising prices and increasing the physical size of its pages. As part of a privately held company, Hearst does not report financial information, but indications are that its willingness to defy conventional wisdom has been working.

The magazines keep much of their printed material offline, although the practice varies widely from one to another. Their sites try to tantalize readers with things that they can see only in print—and drive them to buy subscriptions. Last year, more than one-quarter of new subscriptions were sold through the sites, and this year that could reach one-third.

Though the strategy defies conventional wisdom, Ms. Cathie Black, president of Hearst Magazines, said it seemed fairly obvious.

"I want 1.6 million women to go to the newsstand every month to buy Cosmo, and they do," she said. "We don't want that genie out of the bottle. I don't have any interest in challenging that economic model."

"I give a lot of credit to Hearst for being willing to go in one direction when everyone else is going in the other direction," said Samir Husni, chairman of the journalism department at the University of Mississippi and editor of MrMagazine.com, which follows the industry. "They're doing well in a tough time, and *Food Network* is the big success story of 2009."

Did you ever wonder why very successful privately held companies such as Milliken or Gore-Tex rarely show up in the press? That's because no one is staring at their numbers quarter after quarter. All they have to worry about is their business. And if they are happy with it, that's all that matters.

It reminds me of yet another story. I've published this before, but I can't resist retelling it. It's a classic, and it's always fun to read again.

The Tico Fisherman and the Wall Street Analyst

An American businessman was at the pier of a small coastal Costa Rican village when a small boat with just one fisherman docked. Inside the small boat were several large yellowfin tuna.

The American complimented the Costa Rican Tico on the quality of his fish and asked how long it had taken him to catch them.

The Tico replied, "Only a little while." The American then asked why he didn't stay out longer and catch more fish. The Tico said that he had enough to support his family's immediate needs.

The American then asked, "But what do you do with the rest of your time?"

The Tico fisherman said, "I sleep late, fish a little, play with my children, take siesta with my wife, Maria, and stroll into the village each evening, where I sip wine and play guitar with my amigos. I have a full and busy life, señor."

The American scoffed. "I am a Wall Street executive, and I could help you. You should spend more time fishing and with the proceeds buy a bigger boat and a Web presence. A scalable go-forward plan would provide capital for several new boats. Eventually you would have a fleet of fishing boats. Instead of selling your catch to a middleman, you would sell directly to the processor, eventually opening your own cannery. You would control the product, processing, and distribution. You would need to leave this small coastal fishing village and move to San José, Costa Rica, then to Los Angeles, and eventually to New York City, where you would outsource tasks to third-party clients to help run your expanding enterprise in a vertical market."

The Tico fisherman asked, "But señor, how long will this all take?"

The American replied, "Fifteen to twenty years."

"But what then, señor?"

The American laughed and said, "That's the best part. When the time is right, you will announce an IPO and sell your company stock to the public and become very rich. You will make millions."

"Millions, señor? Then what?"

The American said, "Then you will retire and move to a small coastal fishing village, where you can sleep late, fish a little, play with your kids, take siesta with your wife, and stroll to the village in the evenings, where you will sip wine and play your guitar with your amigos."

PART 3

CRISIS

When you are in a crisis, there is no time to run a study. The prospect of dying has a way of focusing your attention in a big hurry.

—Lee Iacocca

Nothing gets your attention better than a good old crisis. Currently we have two varieties: macro and micro.

The macro variety is the financial crisis that has swept the world. It has almost wiped out a large chunk of the automotive, financial, and retail sectors. How do you operate in this environment?

Then there's the "micro" version of a crisis. This is where the survival of an individual company, such as AIG or GM, is on the line. Whatever crisis you're facing, it's time to fasten your seat belts and hang on.

CHAPTER SEVEN

A CRISIS CAN
CHANGE THE GAME

In many ways, we've gone beyond the unpredictable. We live in the age of the unthinkable. That happens to be the title of a book by Joshua Cooper Ramo that everyone should read. The subtitle pretty much lays out what marketers face: "Why the new world disorder constantly surprises us and what we can do about it."

Recent times have certainly educated us to the fact that we live in a time of uncertainty or crisis. And these crises come in two forms: macro and micro.

The macro variety would be the financial crisis that has swept the world, affecting just about everyone. As previously mentioned, a micro crisis would be one that threatens an entire company, such as GM or AIG. In either case, you wake up one day and find that your world has changed for the worse.

The End of Long-Term Planning

Suddenly, we are faced with the fact that the concept of long-term planning has finally been put to rest. It's already been ridiculed by many. Malcolm Forbes said it very well: "Anyone who says businessmen deal in facts, not fiction, has never read old five-year projections."

A long-term strategic plan is useless unless you include your competitors' plans as well. Yet many CEOs think that complex long-term planning is critical if a company is going to fulfill its mission statement.

If Shakespeare came back as a CEO, he'd be tempted to kill his company's long-term planners as well as its lawyers. And he'd have ample ammunition. Long-term planning didn't make Xerox a factor in office automation. Long-term planning didn't keep GM from losing over 30 points of the automotive market in 30 years.

Where It All Started

It all really began in the early 1960s, when General Electric emerged as the pioneer in strategic planning. GE created a large, centralized staff of planners to ponder the future. Consultant McKinsey & Co. helped GE view its products in terms of strategic business units, identified competitors for each, and evaluated its position against those competitors.

But long-term planning really picked up steam in 1963. Under founder Bruce D. Henderson, Boston Consulting Group (BCG) became the first of many strategy boutiques. BCG pioneered a series of concepts that took corporate America by storm, including the "experience curve" and the "growth and market-share matrix."

Today's enlightened discussion of long-term strategy would include talk about "strategic intent," "white-space opportunities," and "coevolution."

For those of you who've missed the concept of "co-evolving," it talks about "business ecosystems" in which companies work cooperatively and competitively to create the next round of innovation. (This sounds like la-la land to us.)

It all comes out of a book entitled *The Death of Competition*. Our question: If competition has died, who are those folks who are trying to take away our business?

Silly Predictions

Beyond all the nonsense, that fatal flaw in all of this long-term planning is the simple fact that you can't predict the future. History is filled with bold forecasts that didn't pan out. Here's a sampling of predictions that flopped:

- "Airplanes are interesting but of no military value." Marshal Ferdinand Foch, French military strategist, 1911.
- "The horse is here to stay, but the automobile is only a novelty, a fad." President of Michigan Savings Bank, 1903, advising Henry Ford's lawyer not to invest in the Ford Motor Co.
- "What use could this company make of an electrical toy?" Western Union president William Orton, rejecting Alexander Graham Bell's offer to sell his struggling telephone company to Western Union for $100,000.
- "Who the hell wants to hear actors talk?" Harry Warner, Warner Brothers, 1927.
- "We don't like their sound. Groups of guitars are on the way out." Decca Records's statement on rejecting the Beatles, 1962.
- "There is no reason for any individual to have a computer in their home." Kenneth Olsen, founder and president of Digital Equipment Corp., 1977.

So if you can't plan long term or predict the future, what do you do? You have to stay flexible and seize the opportunity.

The Nuclear Energy Crisis

Let's look at the current nuclear energy business as an example of how to handle what has become a macro crisis in the U.S. market for this source of energy.

It all began in the 1960s. General Electric introduced what was the first of the nuclear power plants at Dresden, which was near Chicago. At the time, this was perceived as being the first of a new generation of power plants that was going to be a big deal. To support this effort, GE launched a big consumer educational program entitled Citizen Atom. It laid out all the wonderful things that atomic power was going to accomplish.

But crisis struck first through a movie staring Jane Fonda; then, 12 days after the film's release, at Three Mile Island; and eventually at Chernobyl. Suddenly America was afraid of nuclear power, and many people even had the misguided sense that a nuclear power plant could blow up. When you added that fear to the cost of these plants, the market suddenly dried up along with all those grand plans. It was a full-blown crisis.

Seizing an Opportunity

But that was then. Today there is a lot of talk about alternative energy not based on hydrocarbons. Climate change, Arab oil, and the like have suddenly put nuclear power back in play.

Now is the time to aggressively seize the opportunity to reposition nuclear energy as an alternative fuel of the future. Whether this should be a company or an industry program will have to be determined. In our view, it will have to be a major industry program in order to have enough size and weight behind it. And, in addition to making an effort with consumers, a major effort with Washington will be needed as well. Industry programs are always hard to mobilize, so that has to be the first effort. But now comes the critical decision. How do we get around the fear that these plants can still be dangerous? This calls for some careful repositioning.

Forget the Past

In a rapidly changing world, clinging to the past can be fatal. So it is with the nuclear power industry. To get around the fears out there, the industry has to be willing to shed the word that is at the heart of this fear: *nuclear*. Back when the terms *atomic* and *nuclear* were born, no one ever envisioned them as being anchors that could drag down the industry.

In a repositioning program, these words should be dropped and the industry renamed, as minds will never be changed about the word *nuclear*. The press is alive with that word as it discusses North Korea and Iran. The bomb is still with us.

What makes more sense is to reposition the industry around the *source* of the energy. In other words, energy can be generated by coal, oil, gas, solar, and wind. Why not add uranium to that list of sources? A uranium power plant doesn't sound very dangerous. A uranium power industry certainly sounds a lot friendlier.

The game of repositioning often comes down to selecting the right words because, as you learned in Chapter 1, it's all a battle of perceptions, and words are your weapons.

The GM Crisis

GM is the mother of all micro crises.

Much, and I mean much, has been written about the General Motors crisis. Some claim that the situation is hopeless. Others say that there's a chance that things will work out in time. No one writes about the fact that success or failure will not revolve around the GM brand. (No one walks into a car dealership and asks for a GM car.)

GM's future depends on how well its remaining brands are repositioned and how well each strategy is executed. In some ways, it is a replay of Alfred Sloan's eliminating a number of GM brands and building a gigantic business around five brands that became a "car for every purse and purpose." But that was then. What's available in today's highly saturated and wildly competitive automobile market?

First, what drives today's most successful brands? As you have read earlier in this book, in a word, it's a word. The most powerful brands stand for a word or a concept. Toyota is about reliability. BMW is about drivability. Mercedes is about engineering. Volvo built a brand around safety. The problem with the GM brands was that each of them lacked that simple differentiating idea. This was the result of each brand trying to be everything for everybody. What's a Chevrolet? It's a big, small, expensive, cheap, truck, van, or sports car.

So the task for the postbankrupt GM is to carefully figure out what its four remaining brands should be about. What is the differentiating strategy to pursue?

Interestingly, there are some obvious ideas on the table that the company can move to preempt. Let's start at the bottom, with Chevrolet. If you look at the numbers, Chevrolet has a chance to be repositioned as a leader. This is always a good strategy, as people buy what other people buy. What's a Chevrolet? It's "America's favorite American car." Good value, variety, and heritage can be the story.

Next up is Buick. The first move should be to stop making any cheap Buicks. Don't compete with Chevrolet. What Buick wants to do is compete with the cheap BMWs, Mercedes, and other luxury automobiles that are trying to go down in price to sell more vehicles. This sets up a repositioning idea that a Buick is about "quality without paying for status." That could be a very powerful value story in a world that is buying less status.

Continuing up the ladder, we have Cadillac. This can never be a true prestige car. The fancy imports dominate that category. What Cadillac can stand for is "leading-edge technology" in such things as engine performance, safety, or electronics. Some people love to buy the latest thing.

Finally there is GMC. I'm not sure why the company wants to hang on to this brand, but there is an idea that it could use, especially with the larger vehicles that use this nameplate. The repositioning idea is that of "rugged reliability." It comes out of the prior "professional-grade" promotion of this brand, but it is a lot more meaningful. Of course, the company would have to deliver on that promise.

There you have it. Four brands that are well repositioned in a tough marketplace. One could say that if the company executes properly and stays focused on these concepts, it has a shot at success. If not? Well, let's not drive there.

Some Guidelines

Yes, a crisis can change the game, but there are some underlying guidelines that can always be of help.

We've been in this marketing business for many years, and we have seen the good old times and the difficult new times. When people ask what has changed, our response is one word: *competition*. As you read in Chapter 2, everybody is after everybody else's business, and a crisis only makes things more competitive.

Because of this ugly fact of life, the key to survival is to start every marketing plan with your competition in mind. It's not what you want to do; it's what your competition will let you do. In the next two sections, there are survival tips in a search for a repositioning strategy.

Avoid a Competitor's Strength and Exploit Its Weakness

When a competitor is known for one thing, you have to be known for something else. Quite often, a competitor's built-in weakness is the something else that you can exploit. If McDonald's strength is that of being a little kid's place, Burger King can exploit that by being a grown-up place. For years, Detroit's automobiles were perceived as not being very reliable. Toyota was able to exploit these perceptions and take ownership of the attribute of "reliability."

But remember, we're talking strength and weakness in the minds of the marketplace. Marketing is a battle of perceptions. What you're really doing is exploiting perceptions.

You also have to realize that at least one of your competitors is probably in a meeting right now figuring out how to nail you in one way or another. You must constantly be gathering information on what your competitors are planning. This can come from an astute sales force, from a friendly customer, or from some research.

Never underestimate your competitors. In fact, you're safer if you overestimate them. AT&T, Digital Equipment Corp., Levi's, and Crest are testimony to underestimating the kind of damage that competitors can do, even to market leaders.

Competitors Will Usually Get Better, If Pushed

Companies that figure that they can exploit a sloppy competitor are making a big mistake. They ridicule the competitor's product or service and say that they can do things better. Then, lo and behold, their big competitor suddenly improves and that so-called advantage melts away.

Number two Avis did indeed try harder, but Hertz quickly improved its efforts. Then one day Hertz ran a devastating ad with this headline: "For years, Avis has been telling you they are No. 2. Now we're going to tell you why."

Then Hertz went on to lay out all its improvements. Avis never quite recovered.

Never build your program around your competitors' mistakes. They will correct those mistakes in short order.

CHAPTER EIGHT

VALUE IS THE NAME
OF THE GAME

In Chapter 2, we talked about repositioning the competition as not being about price. When you are talking about value, once again it is not about price unless you have built a price advantage. If that's the case, you are always about price as your differentiator.

Southwest Airlines has used low price to differentiate itself. But it has done so by, in CEO Herb Kelleher's words, "being different."

By using only one kind of airplane, Southwest saved on training and maintenance costs. By offering no reserved seats, it avoided expensive reservation systems. By offering no food, it eliminated expense and time. By avoiding expensive hub airports and using less expensive smaller airports, it avoided high gate charges.

(Southwest has recently moved to a reserved section and bigger hubs, but they are evolving carefully.)

By being different, Southwest has been able to construct a system with the lowest cost per air mile of any airline. Unfortunately, this has turned it into a bit of a cattle car. But to offset this, it works very hard at making the trip more fun. (The attendants do stand-up comedy.)

Southwest has differentiated itself as the low-fare airline. And it has become big enough that it can't be forced out of a market by a bigger airline lowering its prices. Many airlines have tried to imitate Southwest, and most have failed.

The Wal-Mart Success

One could say that the original "everyday low prices" has worked for Wal-Mart in the mass merchandising business. Like Southwest Airlines, Wal-Mart has been able to make low price a meaningful differentiating idea. But consider how the company got there.

First, it began their efforts in America's C and D counties (the ones with smaller populations), where its competition was the small mom-and-pop general-merchandise stores. That was like the German war machine running through the Balkans. There was very little resistance.

Then it began to build its technology base along with its new store openings. As its volumes grew, it added "supplier muscle" to its weapons. While the going has been tougher in areas where Kmart, Target, and Costco also reside, it now indeed has that structural cost advantage to support its claim. Recently it has repositioned itself as being about saving money. That is an improvement, as it gets the company away from comparison shopping. Secret: Wal-Mart's prices are not always the lowest on an item-by-item comparison.

The PC Empire Strikes Back

In the computer wars, edgy Apple has successfully repositioned the PC as being "nerdy" and uncool. This has worked well for the Mac, which has continued to sell well as the PC market slumped during the recession. It set up its "ease of use" and "esthetically pleasing" points of difference. But these benefits can cost you. So in 2009, the PC started fighting back with a better price proposition.

Perky twentysomethings and other average Americans are shown shopping for a computer. One wants a notebook with a 17-inch screen, and if she finds it for less than $1,000, she can keep it. Following her as she shops, we learn that she considers a Mac way too expensive. From the Apple store, it's off to Best Buy, where she finds a PC that meets her specifications for $699. Mission accomplished. She celebrates, saying, "I'm a PC, and I got just what I wanted."

In real life, that bottom line has a little wiggle room. Sure, a $699 PC beats a $2,800 Mac with a 17-inch screen. But the typical customer winds up adding antivirus software and different audio and video software. But so what? You're still paying less than half of what a Mac costs.

While it is not our favorite strategy, price can be a very effective weapon in repositioning, especially in the middle of a crushing recession. A PC might not be cool, but it can save you some money. Point and counterpoint.

Charles Schwab's Approach

Charles Schwab, the company that was the first discount broker, faced a similar situation. It was its price approach that broke the hammerlock that the big full-service brokers had on the market. But this gave way to an army of other discount brokers, who were more recently followed by an army of yet cheaper brokers on the Internet.

Charles Schwab has moved to the high ground with more and more service. While the firm is still about discounts, if you look at its advertising, Charles Schwab looks more and more like Merrill Lynch than Merrill Lynch, the behemoth of costly full-service firms, does. It's even added a bank, which to us is a little confusing.

The moral of the Charles Schwab story is that you can start with price, but unless you have a structural advantage, you can't finish with price. You've got to move up the food chain by adding value. Schwab has done that as it has become a much-admired financial institution.

Getting around Price

Market leaders will always be attacked on price as their competitors try to reposition them as expensive. It appears to be almost a law of nature. So what do you do? Do you have to match all the moves that are made against you?

Well, there are some tried-and-true methods of getting around a price attack.

1. *Do something special.* The leader can go to its biggest customers and offer something special. Nike went to Foot Locker with Tuned Air, a $130 running shoe that it makes exclusively for the big shoe retailer. So far, so good. Foot Locker

has ordered more than a million pairs and expects to sell $200 million worth. That's comparable to what Nike did with the bestselling Air Jordans.

2. *Shift the argument.* Another good value strategy in a pricing battle is to introduce the concept of total cost as opposed to initial cost. In some categories, the costs you incur after you buy a product can be substantial. If your product performs better after the purchase, you might be able to build a cost-of-ownership rather than a cost-of-purchase argument. A variation on this is the concept of longevity. An expensive product, such as a Mercedes, can have a high price, but it will last far longer than your average car. That's a nice rationale to get customers over what could be a bad case of sticker shock. A similar strategy can be used to sell expensive beds such as Duxiana, which go for $3,000 or more. The concept: you spend a lot more time in your bed than in your expensive car. In fact, you spend about 40 percent of your life in bed. So why scrimp?

3. *Add more.* There are times when value is a sum total game. If you can add items to your offer, people will begin to feel that they are getting more for their money. Some years ago, we were asked about

Continental Airlines. It had come out of bankruptcy, had installed new management, and was repositioning itself as a new airline. It had the newest fleet. It had an improved business class and improved club services. It served food (and has continued to do so in recent times, even after other airlines have stopped). It has added more destinations. The obvious strategy was to tell a value story, which we verbalized as "more airline for the money." It used this concept until (you guessed it) a new advertising agency arrived with its idea: "Work hard. Fly right." The value strategy was replaced by a meaningless slogan.

4. *Be nice and helpful.* When you are in a retail, consumer-centric business, service can be a powerful value story. Tucked away in Greenwich, Connecticut, is Sam Bridge Nursery. A full-service, year-round garden center, it's been in business since 1930. It certainly isn't the cheapest place to buy plants and horticultural materials, but it sure is the friendliest. Any elderly lady rolling a wagon full of plants is quickly aided by staff members. Any questions about anything are quickly answered. One shopper asked another why she comes to Bridge. The answer was, "No one else is as nice."

Yes, it takes a lot of effort and cost and training to make your staff nice and helpful, but you'll get it back by being able to charge a little more even in a time of crisis. A paragraph from the Sam Bridge Web site gives you a sense of how hard the company works at giving better service and value:

> Here at Sam Bridge Nursery and Greenhouses we pride ourselves on our superior customer service and knowledgeable staff. We have been providing expert advice to our customers since 1930. Throughout the year our staff attends many industry conferences, trade shows, and open houses to ensure the most current and accurate information is passed onto you. If you have any questions please feel free to call us or stop by and we will be happy to answer it for you.*

Big on Service

There are those who would say that it's easy to be nice when you're a small operation like Sam Bridge Nursery. That's a fair observation, so let's talk about big.

Best Buy, the big-box electronics store, is the last man standing. Its two big competitors, Circuit City

---

* http://www.sambridge.com/staff.html; http://www.sambridge.com/aboutus.html.

and CompUSA, are now gone. The reason is that even in good times, electronics retailing can be a brutally tough business, haunted by thin profit margins, ever-falling prices, feast-or-famine product cycles, and price pressure from Internet retailers. On top of that you have the likes of Wal-Mart and Costco skimming electronics shoppers. This sounds like a case for repositioning.

As reported in the *New York Times*, Brian Dunn, Best Buy's new CEO, plans to reposition the chain around services, something that in the past it has done better than any national electronics retailer. That translates into selling product warranties or help with installing a home theater or configuring a computer. An analyst at Pacific Crest Securities forecasts that such services, which can be highly profitable, could bring in 5 percent of the company's $47 billion in sales in the next fiscal year. The company's blue-shirted tech support staff, called the Geek Squad, has expanded beyond PC-centric services.

Not all of the company's services are direct revenue generators. Dunn said that a chief example of the kind of thing Best Buy wants to be known for is a service it calls Walk Out Working, which it began introducing in May 2007. The service, which is free, helps consumers configure new mobile phones so that when they leave the store, they are able to use features like music play-back and Web surfing.*

This sounds like a pretty good repositioning strategy to us. It's similar to the Sam Bridge story. If one shopper asks another why he comes to Best Buy, and if the answer is, "No one else is as smart," it could be said that the firm's repositioning mission has been accomplished.

Prestige Is Out; Value Is In

These are hard times for expensive brands. What is a brand to do when its customers feel that it is necessary to cut back and save? Or when products that were sold on prestige are not socially acceptable?

Do you cut your prices and thus tell your customers that you were overcharging them? A Vera Wang wedding gown once averaged $5,500. Next year it will be $3,800. She is also introducing a lower-priced casual line called Lavender aimed at twenty- and thirtysomethings. Nordstrom is opening fewer full-price department stores and has tripled the pace of opening lower-price Nordstrom Rack stores. We're not so sure about all these subbrands and their impact on the main brand.

---

* http://www.nytimes.com/2009/07/18/technology/companies/
  18bestbuy.html.

Companies all over the globe are facing this dilemma. One to watch is Coach, a maker of rather expensive ladies handbags. When sales of its $300-plus bags tanked in the middle of the financial crisis, its managers were faced with a decision that made them uncomfortable. As the CEO, Lew Frankfort, recounted, "The first question everyone asked when they came into our full-price stores was, 'What's for sale?'" Frankfort's response was, "We never go on sale. But any lingering resistance to the idea that Coach had to reposition itself ended then." But what to do?

A New Brand

Rather than cut prices, Coach decided to launch a new subbrand that is more youthful, using new materials and new designs. It is to be called the "Poppy" line, and it will sell for an average price of $260, or 20 percent less than the usual Coach purse. We prefer the new-brand strategy over that of just cutting price on existing brands. But your new brand should have its own name, look, and market segment, while still being profitable. And there should be a clear differentiating story between the original brand and the new brand. All this requires a great deal of work and planning. As this is being written, the main pieces of the Poppy collection were tested in 9 Coach stores and 23 department stores.

The bestsellers were $98 bags. Will Coach find happiness selling $300 and $200 handbags? That's still to be determined. But it now has two good horses in the race, instead of one that's carrying too much weight.

Selling Expensive Watches

Sometimes, you just have to suck up your high price and adjust your selling technique.

Nowhere has the financial crisis hit harder than in the land of expensive watches that are collector's items. The worst decline for Swiss watches is in the United States, where sales fell 40 percent from a year earlier.

While sales of expensive watches are way off, business is booming for a Paris-based luxury-sales consulting group called Pôle Luxe. As reported in the *Wall Street Journal,* it's interesting to see that its training encourages salespeople to say "value" rather than "price" and to sell "romance" rather than "products." And don't bargain with clients. The salespeople are coached to offer a gift if a discount is requested, and they have a closet filled with these gifts.

Pôle Luxe has an approach that can be summed up as going like this: "Madam, this timepiece comes from our finest workshop, and it has a value of $10,000. If you buy it, your children are sure to enjoy it for generations to come."

Now that is what we call a nifty piece of repositioning.

Sneaky Sales

Undermining a prestige brand with a lower price can be a daunting problem because high price supports the fact that it is a prestige product. As David Schick, a retailing analyst, said, "When you are selling anything in luxury, you are selling exclusivity."

Rather than posting big sale signs that can mar a store's reputation, high-end chains are telling customers they can buy an item for less even if the price tag says otherwise. These are what I call "sneaky sales." Some have an online-only sales promise to knock 50 percent off luxury goods when you click on a certain link in the message.

Other techniques inform customers of a sale mere hours before it begins. And then there is the discreet offering of discounts only to top customers. Such offers preserve a brand's veneer while delivering a sense of urgency about a value whispered into the ear of a customer.

All these brands realize that once the world sees you go down in price in a very public way, you can never go back up again.

Adding Value to Your Story

Consider the technology of ultrasound, which is up against MRI and CT scanning. Initially these were floor-standing machines, but these are being disrupted by portable machines.

We work with a company called SonoSite, the pioneer and current leader in small, handheld machines. Its strategy is to establish the perception of leadership and drive home its benefit of "big-machine performance in a small machine." That has worked quite well.

But now, even in health care, we have a crisis. Money for any new technology will be difficult to obtain. Here's where a repositioning strategy that deals with this crisis has to be considered. The strategy can be summed up in a simple question and answer:

Q. How did a small machine become a big idea in medicine?

A. By saving time and money while improving patient outcome.

You can see that SonoSite is using repositioning to adjust perceptions about its value and about saving time and money. In crisis times, that should be a powerful reason for hospital administrators to keep buying small ultrasound machines. The basic leadership story is the same, only now we're adding value to the equation.

A similar story can be told about a company called Rackspace. It is also a leader and a specialist in Web site hosting. (It stores and manages Web sites for companies all over the world.) But even in high tech, the world is in crisis mode, and companies are looking to find ways to reduce costs. Rackspace is using new technology to add value to its story of superior service as its position. It is offering "cloud hosting" as a cost-saving offer to some customers. This uses the Web as a distribution system. While it is not for all applications, such as those that require security, it is a money-saving "value" story. It also reenforces the firm's leadership and specialization story by offering a new, lower-cost form of Web hosting as well as traditional forms of service.

Back to the Future

C. F. Martin & Co. is a guitar-making company whose instruments have been favored by music legends, including Elvis Presley, Gene Autry, and Eric Clapton. Despite the company's legendary status, the financial crisis quickly took 20 percent off its sales of 52,000 guitars a year as its inventories of high-end guitars ballooned.

What to do? C. F. Martin simply revived the no-frills guitars that it sold during the 1930s, or the last serious depression. It introduced a solid-wood "1 series," so named for its simplicity. This guitar sells for less than $1,000, which is quite a value when you consider that the firm's guitars generally sell for $2,000 to $3,000. It accomplished this by removing expensive inlays, as its stripped-down 1930s model had done. The company introduced the 1 series in 2008 and promptly sold out its first year's output of 8,000 guitars.

This return-to-basics strategy can be a natural way to reposition a company around value.

Some Words about Promotions

Finally, do price promotions add much value for a brand? Some extensive international work has shown that sales generally go back to where they were once a short-term price promotion is over. The promotion lasts while it lasts. This has long been suspected, but the issue has only recently been systematically tested. Management has often harbored the hope that there might be a positive aftereffect, at least in a particular case.

It is now known that this is not so, and why: A promotion is taken up almost exclusively by the brand's long-term or "loyal" customers. The evidence shows that people seldom buy a strange brand just because its price is cut. They simply avoid paying more than they have to when one of their customary and familiar brands is temporarily on sale.

This is why there are no aftereffects from sales: A promoted brand does not hang on to those new customers who might have first bought it during the sales blip, because there were virtually no such "new customers." What's more, a typical short-term promotion reaches only a few of the brand's existing customers, say 10 or 20 percent. Yet promotions are very costly, and additionally, they have costly side effects on production and distribution logistics.

Promotions do not seem to leave memory traces. ("What brand had 20 cents off six or so months ago?") Consumers seem to accept the idea that prices are sometimes cut (even for a BMW, say, or for air miles for first class).

Large-scale promotions now occur even though management has traditionally sought to stop its salespeople from cutting the price. ("The only way I could nail the sale, sir.") Marketing management itself now cuts the price, and even seems proud of it. Nonetheless, price promotions must generally be run at a loss; if they weren't there would be even more of them. And the bigger the promotional blip, the bigger the loss.

So why is so much spent on price promotions? Senior management would like to cut its promotional budget but usually does not know how to do so or what will happen if it does.

The exception was the unknown CEO who said, "If you're not sure, all you need is guts."

PART 4

THE ART OF REPOSITIONING

If the blind lead the blind,
both shall fall into the ditch.

—Matthew 15:14

Repositioning sounds easy, but it is not. Readjusting perceptions is a slow process, and it often requires a great deal of courage on the part of top managers. They have to convince themselves, their employees, and, often, a board of directors. And the CEO must often lead the charge and act as a cheerleader. You must be optimistic about success.

There was no one better at this than Herb Kelleher, the founder of Southwest Airlines. It's the reason that Southwest is America's most successful airline. He knew exactly where he was flying.

CHAPTER NINE

REPOSITIONING
TAKES TIME

It is critical to remind readers here that repositioning is about readjusting people's perceptions, not changing their perceptions. The marketplace is littered with failed efforts to change people's minds. Xerox lost hundreds of millions of dollars trying to convince people that Xerox could make computers and other machines that didn't make copies. Coke blew prestige and money in an effort to convince the market that its New Coke was better than the Real Thing. Cadillac tried to convince the market that its small versions were as good as its big versions, first with the Cimarron, then with the Catera. Both were disasters because a Cadillac that looks like a Chevrolet makes no sense. It's important to understand why changing people's minds is so difficult.

Minds Are Hard to Change

There's always been a general feeling in the marketing industry that new-product advertising should generate higher interest than advertising for established brands.

But it turns out that we're actually more impressed by what we already know (or buy) than by what's "new."

One research organization, McCollum Spielman, has tested more than 22,000 TV commercials over 23 years. Almost 6,000 of those commercials were for new products in 10 product categories.

What did McCollum Spielman learn? Greater persuasion ability and attitude shifts—the so-called new-product excitement—were evident in only one of the 10 categories (pet products) when comparing new brands to established brands.

In the other nine categories, ranging from drugs to beverages to personal hygiene items, there was no real difference—no burst of excitement enabling consumers to distinguish between established brands and new brands.

Since thousands of different commercials across hundreds of different brands were tested, you can pretty much rule out creativity as the difference in persuasion. It comes back to what we're familiar with, what we're already comfortable with.

Trying to Change Attitudes

In the book *The Reengineering Revolution*, MIT professor turned consultant Michael Hammer calls human beings' innate resistance to change "the most perplexing, annoying, distressing, and confusing part" of reengineering.

To help us better understand this resistance, a book titled *Attitudes and Persuasion* offers some insights. Written by Richard Petty and John Cacioppo, it spends some time on "belief systems." Here's their take on why minds are so hard to change:

> The nature and structure of belief systems is important from the perspective of an informational theorist, because beliefs are thought to provide the cognitive foundation of an attitude. In order to change an attitude, then, it is presumably necessary to modify the information on which that attitude rests. It is generally necessary, therefore, to change a person's beliefs, eliminate old beliefs, or introduce new beliefs.*

And you're going to do all that with a 30-second commercial?

* Richard E. Petty and John T. Cacioppo, *Attitudes and Persuasion: Classic and Contemporary Approaches* (Boulder, CO: Westview Press, 1996), p. 184.

What Psychologists Say

The Handbook of Social Psychology reinforces how tough it is to change attitudes:

> Any program to change attitudes offers formidable problems. The difficulty of changing a person's basic beliefs, even through so elaborate and intense a procedure as psychotherapy, becomes understandable, as does the fact that procedures that are effective in changing some attitudes have little effect on others.

And what makes things even worse is that truth has no real bearing on these issues. Check out this observation:

> People have attitudes on a staggeringly wide range of issues. They seem to know what they like (and especially dislike) even regarding objects about which they know little, such as Turks, or which have little relevance to their daily concerns, like life in outer space.

So, to paraphrase an old TV show, if your assignment, Mr. Phelps, is to change people's minds, don't accept the assignment.

What "Readjusting" Entails

Now that we've thrown cold water on the idea of changing people's minds, let's focus on readjusting perceptions in the mind by starting with a dictionary definition of *adjust*: to change so as to match or fit.

Matching or fitting with perceptions is what effective repositioning is about. Trying to change a person's mind is the opposite, as you are going against that person's existing perceptions. It is a total mismatch. For example, because Xerox is known as a document company, it could easily reposition itself as a digital document engineering company as a way to preempt the growing popularity of digital storage and distribution of documents. To better understand how this works, let me reprise an old case study with some insights and timing added to the story.

Once upon a time, a company called Lotus Development invented a piece of software that turned a standalone PC into a real business tool. The software was Lotus 1-2-3, and it was the first spreadsheet software. It was a very a big deal at the time. But time and technology moved on and threatened the world of Lotus. A new operating system called Microsoft Windows appeared, and before 1-2-3 could adapt to this very popular operating system, Microsoft introduced a competitive spreadsheet designed for Windows called

Excel. And if that wasn't bad enough, the PC world was trending from stand-alone PCs to networks of PCs, all of which required new kinds of software. This looked like a case for repositioning.

Readjusting Perceptions of Lotus

The new term for software for networked PCs was *groupware,* or software for groups of computers, as coined by *Business Week* magazine in an article on this networking trend. Interestingly Lotus owned the first groupware product, called Notes. That set the stage for a repositioning strategy that we verbalized as: "First the spreadsheet. Now groupware."

By starting off the statement with what was already in people's minds, we were able to establish that fit and make the readjustment. But all this took a great deal of time. To be specific, moving from "spreadsheet" to "groupware" as a position took a good four years of publicity, advertising, and intense management. The CEO told us that he had to fire a number of people who weren't happy with this repositioning strategy. And his fights with the board weren't easy. But time and money heal all wounds, as IBM arrived and paid $3.5 billion for Lotus and Notes. A happy ending to a repositioning story.

It's Never Too Early to Start

Considering the amount of time it takes to readjust perceptions, starting early on figuring things out can be a big advantage. Just such an activity is under way at Netflix, the folks who mail all those DVDs in those red envelopes. Reed Hastings, the CEO of Netflix, thinks his core business will be doomed in four years, as more and more movies will be distributed online rather than by the post office. Thus the problem, which is shared by companies across the entertainment and technology landscape: how to profit from Internet video. What makes Hastings's future so uncertain is that as he repositions Netflix from the DVD rental business to video services business, he will have a large number of new competitors, such as Apple, Amazon, and Google, instead of just Blockbuster.

We'll see how this all works out, but at least Hastings is on the case well before anything hits the fan.

Building a Cyber Island

Talking about time, how about transforming a country's entire economic base?

That's the repositioning effort that's now underway on the island paradise of Mauritius. One of the world's largest shipping ports, Mauritius is strategically located near both India and Africa, and it is a common stopover for ships traveling to or from Asia.

Its economy is dominated by sugarcane, tourism, and shipping. A few years back, a newly elected prime minister determined that this was an opportune time to capitalize on the emerging global digital economy. The primary obstacle, however, was determining how the government could best stimulate entrepreneurship.

In effect, the question came down to: What does it take to transform an entire economy?

- First, a joint venture consisting of the nation's four largest corporations along with the government formed a new corporation to stimulate entrepreneurship and the creation of new companies.
- After acquiring $100 million in corporate and international funding, the government began an ambitious countrywide technology initiative with the launching of an interactive government portal known as Mauritius Government Online or M-GO!
- The government then began putting in place the high-speed telephones, prewired buildings, and other infrastructure necessary to support a wide range of technology start-ups. This effort, combined with the country's multilingual workforce,

positions the country to attract businesses seeking access to customers in India, Africa, and Asia.

- Mauritius invested in the first 3G network in Africa, making possible services like streaming mobile TV and remote video camera surveillance. It plans to move beyond 3G to an even higher-speed service.
- Also coming on stream is a wireless solution that needs no mobile or even landline. You can buy a modem that uses the emerging Wimax technology. It plugs straight into your PC and receives its signal from a Wimax base station a couple of kilometers away. Wimax has been described as "Wi-Fi on steroids," with hot spots often spanning several kilometers.

Five years into the transformation, the BBC reported in 2008, "For a country which has built its wealth largely on tourism and sugarcane, this is a radical change of direction."

You can see the evidence in a 12-story Cyber Tower that is home to a cluster of tech-oriented companies—in one corner software developers; in another, remote data storage facilities for companies and even countries making sure their data are in safe hands.

Interviewed by the BBC, the prime-minister-turned-president who laid the foundations of the whole Cyber Island concept said:

> There was lots of criticism; that it was not going to help Mauritius, that it was a waste of time. Some people were even saying that I was putting up a white elephant that was going to be a burden to the economy of the country. I didn't listen to all this. But I convinced them that we should go forward. And now it's growing and we can make a cyber island of Mauritius.*

Repositioning Needs Publicity

Another reason that this process takes time is that you need others to write about your efforts. And, as you would expect, this will not happen overnight. The Lotus move to groupware took years of stories in a wide variety of business media. This form of third-party endorsement is necessary for credibility. You can claim that you are changing, but no one will believe you, as it is just a claim. When others report that you are changing, it is a different story. But these kinds of stories are hard to come by, so our advice is that PR should be-

* http://news.bbc.co.uk/2/hi/programmes/click_online/7169467.stm.

come a critical part of your marketing efforts. So here is a list of dos and don'ts about this process.

Advertising Second

Since unplanned, untimely exposure dulls the publicity potential of a repositioning concept, it's easy to see that advertising has to be handled carefully if a company wants to take maximum advantage of PR. Never run ads until the major publicity possibilities have been exploited.

The general rule is: publicity first, advertising second. (PR plants the seed. Advertising harvests the crop.)

The truth is, advertising cannot start a fire. It can only fan a fire that has already been started. To get something going from nothing, you need the validity that third-party endorsements bring. The first stage of any new campaign ought to be public relations.

When a company is using repositioning as its basic advertising strategy, then it just makes sense to use a repositioning strategy in PR. Especially since the PR ought to precede the advertising.

Too often, this doesn't happen. Advertising agencies and public relations agencies see themselves as competitors—for the client's ear and for his dollar.

This intramural rivalry saps the strength of many product and corporate programs. The advertising runs too soon and kills much of the PR potential. Or the PR lacks a positioning concept, so it doesn't set up anything that the advertising can exploit.

What's needed is a basic change in the way advertising and public relations programs are planned. Programs must be developed that are linear rather than spatial.

Quick Bang vs. Slow Buildup

In a spatial program, the elements start together, but in different spaces (public relations, advertising, sales promotion, and so on). This is the typical way most programs are conceived. The quick bang, if you will.

But when the smoke clears away, when the excitement of the initial launch is over, usually nothing has been changed. The prospect's attitude is the same as it was before.

In a linear program, the elements unfold over a period of time. The advantage, of course, is that they can be designed to work together to reinforce each other. The slow buildup leads to a big change in the prospect's mind.

The trouble with most spatial programs is that they don't go anywhere. There's no buildup, no climax, no unfolding of elements, no drama, no "what's going to happen next" excitement.

This is why the beginning of a new year usually marks the start of a new spatial strategy, a new advertising theme.

This annual changeover is just the opposite of good repositioning strategy. More than anything else, successful repositioning requires consistency. You must keep at it, year after year after year.

A linear program helps you achieve this consistency. The gradual buildup of an idea or concept allows plenty of time for the public relations portion of the program to be developed to its fullest extent.

The Mass-Is-Best Trap

There is a tendency on the part of the publicist to shoot for the moon—to try to place a story first in the biggest, most massive media. But this overlooks the linear nature of good public relations strategy. A story in the *Wall Street Journal* is the end of a good PR program, not the beginning.

What works best is starting with your core group and then rolling it out. A story on a well-read blog ("Web log" to the uninitiated) leads to one in a trade publication, which improves your chances of getting one in a general business magazine. Then you can move on to a consumer publication and ultimately to network television, with a few side trips along the way to radio and newspapers if they make sense.

If you can win the battle with the core group first, your future success is almost automatically assured.

Bypassing Old Media

What's happening in the PR world is that a group of bloggers and Twitterers are becoming the focus of early PR. This is especially true in the high-tech world of Silicon Valley. The online pundits are useful, as they can add a level of credibility to any start-up. In the old days, companies courted the early adopters who talked up a new product to their friends and neighbors. Today, that crowd can be found online, not talking up your product over the back fence. This group will eventually lead your story into the trade press and, if you're lucky, on to the business press.

But beware: great press does not a great success make. A lot of dot-coms never make it because they can't figure out how to make money. Consider Segway, the gyroscopic scooter. Enormous press; little in the way of sales. The reason? Where do you go with this product? In the street? That's dangerous. On sidewalks? That's dangerous, too. And then there is the looking silly factor. Nothing looks as goofy as someone riding alone on one of those scooters. Totally uncool.

Four Rules for Success

If this discussion has motivated you to take a closer look at your public relations program, here are some simple rules that can serve as a starting point.

1. Find out what position you already have in your public's mind. Spend a few dollars for research. Or put on your hat and coat and go out and talk to customers and prospects. And don't forget the most important people of all: the editors of your key publications.

2. Adopt a repositioning strategy that you want to own. Zero in on the specific concept that you want to achieve through public relations and advertising. Make sure this idea is not a general one, like improving your image. And avoid attributes like *dynamic, modern,* or *progressive.* These are not about repositioning; they are purely a question of style that public relations can seldom do much about.

3. Convince everyone to concentrate exclusively on this one repositioning approach. This includes your management, your advertising agency, and, of course, everyone in your public relations department. Stick to your one basic strategy, and reinforce it with every press and public penetration.

4. From time to time, evaluate your PR efforts along with your advertising, merchandising, and overall marketing positions. Public relations is simply one of a number of tools that should all be aiming in the same direction. It is self-defeating when PR pulls in one direction and advertising in another.

Remember, readjusting perceptions takes time and patience.

CHAPTER TEN

REPOSITIONING IS NOT FOR THE MEEK

Someone has to be in charge of repositioning. And that type of leadership takes a lot of courage. The role of the CEO is to lead the charge, a point I make in the last chapter of many of my books. Strategy, vision, and mission statements are dependent on the simple premise that you must know where you're going. No one can follow you if you don't know where you're headed.

Since repositioning entails a basic change in your marketing strategy, you would assume top management involvement, which often is not the case. General Motors Vice Chairman Bob Lutz summed up the problem brilliantly in a *Business Week* interview. "To spend $200 million on manufacturing, we have to get board approval with top management involved from an early stage. Yet we spend billions on marketing and delegate that to too many people at the lowest levels. It's insanity."*

This reminds me of a famous David Packard (of Hewlett-Packard) quote: "Marketing is too important to be left to the marketing people."

Many years ago, in a book called *The Peter Principle*, authors Peter and Hull made this observation:

> Most hierarchies are nowadays so cumbered with rules and traditions, and so bound in by public laws, that even high employees do not have to lead anyone anywhere, in the sense of pointing out the direction and setting the pace. They simply follow precedents, obey regulations, and move at the head of the crowd. Such employees lead only in the sense that the carved wooden figurehead leads the ship.†

Perhaps this pessimistic view of leadership skills has led to the explosion of hundreds of books dealing with leadership (most of them downright silly). There's advice on whom to emulate (Attila the Hun), what to achieve (inner peace), what to study (failure), what to strive for (charisma), whether to delegate (sometimes),

* David Kiley, "Bob Lutz, GM Salesman," *BusinessWeek*, August 3, 2009.
† Laurence J. Peter and Raymond Hull, *The Peter Principle* (New York: William Morrow, 1969), p. 68.

whether to collaborate (maybe), America's secret leaders (women), the personal qualities of leadership (having integrity), how to achieve credibility (be credible), how to be an authentic leader (find the leader within), the nine natural laws of leadership (don't even ask). In fact, the last time I counted, there were 3,098 books in print with the word *leader* in the title.

To us, how to be an effective leader isn't worth a whole book. Peter Drucker gets it into a few sentences. "The foundation of effective leadership is thinking through the organization's mission, defining it and establishing it, clearly and visibly. The leader sets the goals, sets the priorities, and sets and maintains the standards."*

The Proper Direction?

First, how do you find the proper direction? To become a great strategist, you have to put your mind in the mud of the marketplace. You have to find your inspiration down at the front, in the ebb and flow of the great marketing battles that are taking place in the mind of the prospect.

Alfred P. Sloan built General Motors into the world's leading manufacturing entity in the 1930s. But he defied

* Peter Drucker, "More Doing than Dash," *Wall Street Journal*, January 6, 1988.

the typical notion of a chairman because he liked to actually work with customers. Every so often, Sloan would disappear from Detroit headquarters and show up at a dealer's lot in another city. He would introduce himself and ask the dealer's permission to work as an assistant service manager, or as a salesman, for a few days. (Not surprisingly, the dealers always said yes.)

The next week, Sloan would be back in Detroit, firing off memos on customer behavior and customer preferences on everything from dealers to auto styling.

Peter Drucker, the high priest of management thinking, has argued that by working in the field regularly, Sloan spotted more trends and more important trends than customer research did—and spotted them earlier.

It's no secret that most of the world's greatest military strategists started at the bottom. And they maintained their edge by never losing touch with the realities of war. Karl von Clausewitz did not attend the best military schools and did not learn his profession from his superiors. Clausewitz learned his military strategy the best way and the hardest way—by serving in the front lines at some of the bloodiest and most famous battles in military history.

The unpretentious Sam Walton traveled to the front lines of every one of his Wal-Mart stores throughout his life. He even spent time on the loading docks in the middle of the night, talking with the crews.

Unlike "Mister Sam," many chief executives tend to lose touch. The bigger the company, the more likely it is that the chief executive has lost touch with the front lines. This might be the single most important factor limiting such companies' ability to deal with competition, change, and crisis.

Big Is a Problem

All the other factors favor size. Marketing is war, and the first principle of warfare is the principle of force. The larger army, or the larger company, has the advantage. But the larger company gives up some of that advantage if it cannot keep itself focused on the marketing battle that is taking place in the mind of the customer. As you read earlier, big is hard to manage.

The shootout at General Motors between Roger Smith and Ross Perot illustrated the point. When he was on the GM board, Ross Perot spent his weekends buying cars. He was critical of Roger Smith for not doing the same.

"We've got to nuke the GM system," Perot said. He advocated atom-bombing the heated garages, chauffeur-driven limousines, and executive dining rooms. He was right, but it took bankruptcy to blow things up. (What ever happened to Ross?)

Chauffeur-driven limousines for a company that's trying to sell cars? Top management's disconnection from the marketplace is the biggest problem facing big business.

Facts Are a Problem

If you're a busy CEO, how do you gather objective information on what is really happening? How do you get around the propensity of middle managers to tell you what they think you want to hear? How do you get the bad news as well as the good?

If you don't get the bad news directly, bad ideas can flourish instead of being killed. Consider the following parable, which I've written about before, but which is worth republishing:

The Plan

In the beginning was the Plan.

And then came the Assumptions.

And the Assumptions were without form.

And the Plan was completely without substance.

The Workers

And the darkness was upon the face of the workers as they spake unto their Group Head saying:

"It is a crock of shit and it stinketh."

The Group Heads

And the Group Heads went unto their Section Heads and sayeth:

"It is a pail of dung and none may abide the odor thereof."

The Section Heads

And the Section Heads went unto their Managers and sayeth unto them:

"It is a container of excrement. And it is very strong. Such that none may abide it."

The Managers

And the Managers went unto their Director and sayeth unto him:

"It is a vessel of fertilizer. And none may abide its strength."

The Director

And the Director went unto the Vice President and sayeth unto him:

"It promoteth growth and is very powerful."

The Vice President

And the VP went unto the President and sayeth unto him:

"This powerful new Plan will actively promote the growth and efficiency of the Company."

The Policy

And the President looked upon the Plan and saw that it was good, and the Plan became Policy.

One possibility of finding out what's really going on is "going in disguise," or poking around unannounced. This would be especially useful at the distributor or retailer level.

An Example

Thomas Stemberg, the founder of Staples, believed in seeing the world from ground level. He shopped his stores like a customer. He would ask questions that a customer would ask, like, "Where can I find a printer cartridge #96A?"

In many ways this is analogous to the king who dresses up as a commoner and mingles with his subjects. The reason: to get honest opinions on what's happening.

Like kings, chief executives rarely get honest opinions from their ministers. There's just too much intrigue going on at the court.

The members of the sales force, if you have one, are a critical element in the equation. The trick is getting a good, honest evaluation of the competition out of them. The best thing you can do is praise honest information.

Once the word gets around that a CEO prizes honesty and reality, a lot of good information will be forthcoming.

Time Is a Problem

Another aspect of the problem is the allocation of your time. Quite often it is taken up with too many activities that keep you from visiting the front. Too many boards, too many committees, too many testimonial dinners. According to one survey, the average CEO spends 30 percent of her time on "outside activities." She spends another 17 hours a week preparing for meetings.

Since the typical top executive works 61 hours a week, that leaves roughly 20 hours for everything else, including managing the operation and going down to the front.

No wonder chief executives delegate the marketing function. But that's a mistake.

Marketing is too important to be turned over to an underling. If you delegate anything, you should delegate the chairmanship of the next fund-raising drive. The next thing to cut back on is meetings. Instead of talking things over, go out and see for yourself. As General Secretary Gorbachev told President Reagan on the occasion of the president's first trip to the

Soviet Union, "It is better to see once than to hear a hundred times."

You have to put your mind on the tactics of the battle you want to win. You have to focus on your competitors and their strengths and weaknesses in people's minds. You have to search out that one attribute or differentiating idea that will work in the mental battleground.

Then you have to be willing to focus all your efforts to develop a coherent strategy to exploit that repositioning idea.

Change Inside

You also have to be willing to make changes inside the organization in order to exploit the opportunities on the outside.

And you must be a doer. The way to spot a nonleader quickly is to watch for "should." When a viable suggestion is presented, the would-be leader says, "We should do that." Usually, you discover, those "shoulds" pile up and little gets done.

The best leaders share their wisdom with the next generation. Noel Tichy, professor at the University of Michigan Business School, says, "Great leaders have to be great teachers." He estimates that Jack Welch, GE's revered chairman and CEO, devoted 30 percent of his time to leadership development. (Welch even taught at GE's executive training institute once a week.) "That's where he got his leverage," claims Professor Tichy.

Ironically, history shows that Welch lost his leverage by putting GE into financial businesses that crashed during our financial crisis. I'm afraid Welch was seduced by Wall Street and his stock price.

The best leaders know that direction alone is no longer enough. The best leaders are storytellers, cheerleaders, and facilitators. They reinforce their sense of direction or vision with words and action.

There was no greater leader in the airline business than Herb Kelleher, the chairman of Southwest Airlines. He became the king of the low-fare, short-haul airline business. Year after year, his airline is on every list of the "most admired" and "most profitable" companies.

If you've flown Southwest, you've probably recognized the incredible spirit and enthusiasm of the airline personnel. They even have a sense of humor that, as one passenger put it, "makes flying on that cattle car enjoyable."

Anybody who knew Herb realizes that the airline's personality retains Herb's personality. He was an amazing cheerleader who kept those planes moving and morale high. He was indeed "walking behind them."

He also knew his people and his business. In a meeting with Herb, I encouraged him to buy one of the East Coast shuttles that were for sale. It would have instantly made Southwest a big player in the East.

He thought for a minute and said, "I sure would like their gates in New York, Washington, and Boston. But what I don't want is their airplanes and, more importantly, their people."

He sure was right. Cheerleading those East Coast shuttle people would have been impossible.

Personifying a Business

Herb Kelleher also exemplifies another attribute of our best leaders: they tend to live the business and come to personify it. In the heyday of Chase Manhattan Bank, its chairman, David Rockefeller, created news just by visiting foreign heads of state. In effect, he was a head of state.

In his prime, Lee Iacocca personified Chrysler.

Bill Gates still personifies Microsoft. He looks like a computer nerd. He sounds like a computer nerd. He lives in a computer nerd's house.

While everyone knows Bill Gates, very few people know Dino Cortopassi. He is the king of "real Italian tomato sauce," which he supplies to the 60,000 or so real Italian pizzerias and restaurants in America—the red sauce places.

Dino has come to personify "real Italian," which is his differentiating idea. He lives in an Italian villa. He makes sausage. He has vineyards. He has his own bocce court. Every year he goes to Italy to visit his relatives. He sends his important customers the family's olive oil. Just as Gates dominates the software world, Dino dominates the market for fresh-packed tomatoes and sauce.

A visible leader is a very powerful weapon with customers and prospects. This kind of leader offers unique credentials for a company. (The Germans had a deep respect for George Patton—so much so that the Allies used him as a decoy.)

Also, the troops are proud to follow this kind of leader into battle. They trust him instinctively. Without trust, there won't be any followers. And without followers, you won't have much of a charge.

Finally, if you're acting like a general, it's important that you adopt the qualities of a good general.

- *You must be flexible.* You must be flexible to adjust the strategy to the situation, not vice versa. A good general has built-in biases, but he will seriously consider all alternatives and points of view before making a decision.

- *You must have mental courage.* At some point in time, your open mind has to close and a decision must be made. A good general reaches deep inside to find the strength of will and mental courage to prevail.
- *You must be bold.* When the time is right, you must strike quickly and decisively. Boldness is an especially valuable trait when the tide is running with you. That's when to pour it on. Beware of those who exhibit too much courage when the deck is stacked against them. Unfortunately, boldness becomes rarer, the higher the rank.
- *You must know the facts.* A good general builds strategy from the ground up, starting with the details. When the strategy is developed, it will be simple but powerful.
- *You need to be lucky.* Luck can play a large part in any success, provided you can exploit it. And when your luck runs out, you ought to be prepared to cut your losses quickly. "Capitulation is not a disgrace," said Clausewitz. "A general can no more entertain the idea of fighting to the last man than a good chess player would play an obviously lost game."

Off We Go

Some years ago, a presentation on a repositioning strategy was given to John Schnatter of Papa John's fame. In the room were John's marketing people and senior executives. I finished the presentation, and John looked around the room and asked for opinions. As often happens in meetings like this, a lot of people started to pick the strategy apart. After 15 minutes of this, John said, "All right, I've listened to you all, and I have a question. Does anyone here have a better idea?" As you can guess, there was nothing but silence. John, not being meek about anything, said to his staff, "All right, 'Better ingredients. Better pizza.' it is. Off we go."

His people knew where he was going, and they've been following that strategy for years with great success.

CHAPTER ELEVEN

REPOSITIONING BEGINS AND ENDS WITH THE CEO

Since we wrote about leadership in the previous chapter, let's talk about the leader's involvement.

In one of our many strategic meetings at one of America's largest companies, a young lady presented me with what we consider one of the most important pieces of advice I have ever received about positioning.

At the end of a presentation, she came over and offered congratulations on what she thought was an excellent piece of thinking.

But then she startled me by saying that we would never sell any of our repositioning ideas. When I asked why, she replied with a simple but brilliant observation: "You'll never have the right people in the room."

She went on to explain that the top people don't go to meetings like this. And powerful ideas always clash with someone's personal agenda. This ensures an early demise for any concept that has to work its way up the organization for final approval.

Boy, was she right. Over the years, we've learned that brilliant thinking never wins the day on its own merits. If you don't have the right people in the room, effective positioning or repositioning becomes a long shot at best.

Old Cash Cows

The first type of obstacle a repositioning idea will often encounter is an old cash cow. New ideas tend to be built on new opportunities, which can sometimes challenge old businesses. The result is a reluctance to foster the new ideas. Peter Drucker calls this "slaughtering tomorrow's opportunity on the altar of yesterday."

In a meeting at IBM, we were encouraging the company to position its new line of workstations as PMs, or Personal Mainframes. This obviously would have upset the head of the mainframe business, a business that was still throwing off big profits. At the other end of the spectrum, the head of the personal computer business probably would have complained as well.

Only the CEO could have made the decision to pursue a concept that potentially could have attacked his biggest cash cow. And since he wasn't in the room, he never had a chance to consider a strategy that today looks pretty good, when you consider the industry trend toward desktop machines.

The most successful companies are quite good at attacking their cash cows. Gillette is a prime example. First it slaughtered its single-edge and stainless blades with the highly successful twin-bladed razor (Trac II). Then it attacked that idea with an adjustable twin-bladed razor (Atra). Then came the shock-absorbing razor (Sensor). Then the company came up with a sensor with fins. It's called Sensor Excel. Then it was on to the multiblade razors, Mach 3 (three blades) and Fusion (five blades). If Gillette comes up with a better idea, it will reposition its older blades as being obsolete.

"At Gillette, there is no such concept as getting ahead of oneself," concludes Booz & Company, the global consulting firm. "New products go on the drawing board as much as a decade before they are introduced."*

Now consider the less than successful companies. Xerox invented laser printing but never exploited it. Kodak invented digital photography, but it never got out of the laboratories. Watching the decline of film, you know why.

---

* Glenn Rifkin, "Anatomy of Gillette's Latest Global Launch," *Strategy+Business*, Second Quarter 1999, p. 84.

Old Bad Decisions

Another problem with not having the right people in the room is the ghost of old bad decisions. New strategies often clash with prior decisions. In many years of strategic work, no one has ever said, "We're glad you've arrived. We've been doing nothing while we've been waiting for you to get here." Obviously people have been doing a lot, some of which wasn't working very well. (People don't call you when things are good.)

Unfortunately, no one in a large corporation wants to admit to making a bad decision. Especially a bad *big* decision. This is particularly true in an organization that isn't very good at tolerating failure. As a result, it goes against almost all middle-level managers' instincts to embrace any new idea that could cause them embarrassment about their old decisions.

"I'm in Charge Here"

Another problem you may encounter is the "corporate ego" of your immediate superiors or the people at your advertising agency. They may have a problem with an outsider doing their job. "After all," they'll say to themselves, "*I'm* in charge. If I accept someone else's thinking, my superiors will think less of me."

This can be a very difficult situation. We've discovered that, rather than dismissing an "outside" recommendation out of hand, this type of person invariably adds his own thinking to the situation. Makes his contribution, so to speak. What results is a modified strategy that isn't really the same. It's like changing a cake's recipe. It may look the same, but it sure doesn't taste like the same cake. (Advertising agencies are especially good at this kind of modification.)

The higher you are presenting in an organization, the less likely you are to come across this kind of ego problem.

Advice for the Cautious

If, for some reason, getting the right people in the room isn't feasible, you'll have to find a way to get the CEO involved in the process. Without that involvement, your strategy will never be implemented properly. So the trick is to carefully construct a case that your hearers' superiors can be comfortable with as they carry it upward to the CEO.

For example, you might include what I call the "world has changed" section at the beginning of your presentation. This automatically communicates the idea that when the earlier decisions were taken, whether they turned out to be right or wrong, they appeared correct at that time.

The purpose of this kind of language is to soothe egos by masking the earlier mistake. Also, the notion of a changing world makes the decision sound more like one that the CEO should take a look at.

But this may not be enough.

Do Some Educating

Chances are the CEO isn't a marketing person by training, so you'll have to find a way to bring her up to speed.

We've seen two effective ways to do this. The first is to set up a lecture on the subject and invite the top management. Bring in an outside expert, but make sure that part of the session deals with your firm's current problems or opportunities. The other way is to send your CEO a book or two on the subject, pointing out why it is apropos to the problems the company faces.

The book of ours that seems to best fill the bill is *Differentiate or Die*. That appears to be something that CEOs quickly grasp. I suspect the world *Die* has something to do with its popularity.

One final thought. Make sure the CEO is aware of the following Peter Drucker quote:

> Because the purpose of business is to create a customer, the business enterprise has two—and only these two— basic functions: marketing and innovation. Marketing and

innovation produce results; all the rest are costs. Marketing is the *distinguishing*, unique function of the business.*

Use an Analogy

Rather than just tossing that terrifying-looking repositioning decision onto the table, you might want to consider prefacing it with an analogous case study drawn from somewhere in corporate history.

That way, you're saying, "XYZ Company passed on trying something similar, and bad things happened to it." Don't forget to add, "Of course, that may not happen to us."

Believe me, when confronted with someone else's mistakes, people get a lot more objective. The person you're presenting to will say to himself, "With my luck, that *will* happen to us. I'd better show this to the boss."

Implement Slowly

Finally, implement any difficult strategy slowly, especially if it's of the "repositioning" kind.

People need time to adjust to change. By making changes slowly, you reduce the anxiety that comes with a dramatic shift of strategy.

* Peter F. Drucker, *Management: Tasks, Responsibilities, Practices* (New York: Harper & Row, 1974), p. 61.

As someone once said: "Most people can survive the old way. Most people can survive the new way. It's the *transition* that'll kill you."

Many years ago, with my ex-partner, Al Ries, we advised Burger King to hang "Kiddieland" on McDonald's and reposition Burger King as the place for grown-up kids. This would have meant sacrificing a part of the market to McDonald's, not to mention eliminating swing sets from its franchisees' facilities.

This represented a major shift in strategy, and it created instant anxiety. The only way to sell this idea was on a "test it and roll it out slowly" basis. Unfortunately, anxiety won out over "slowly," and an opportunity was missed.

This all points to the inescapable fact that repositioning is serious stuff. It sets a new direction for a company's business strategy. And when serious decisions are being made, top management must be in the room.

Organize for Change

Since we are talking about top management and its involvement, it's fitting to end this chapter with some additional Peter Drucker management advice on repositioning. As you can see, taking his advice certainly calls for having the right people in the room.

One thing is certain for developed countries—and probably for the entire world—we face long years of profound changes. An organization must be organized for constant change. It will no longer be possible to consider entrepreneurial innovation as lying outside of management or even as peripheral to management. Entrepreneurial innovation will have to become the very heart and core of management. The organization's function is entrepreneurial, *to put knowledge to work*—on tools, products, and processes; on the design of work; on *knowledge* itself.

Deliberate emphasis on innovation may be needed most where technological changes are least spectacular. Everyone in a pharmaceutical company knows that the company's survival depends on its ability to replace three quarters of its products by entirely new ones every ten years. But how many people in an insurance company realize that the company's growth—perhaps even it s survival—depends on the development of new forms of insurance? The less spectacular or prominent technological change is in a business, the greater the danger that the whole organization will ossify, and the more important, therefore, is the emphasis on innovation.*

---

* Peter F. Drucker with Joseph A. Maciariello, *The Daily Drucker* (New York, Harper Business, 2004), p. 77.

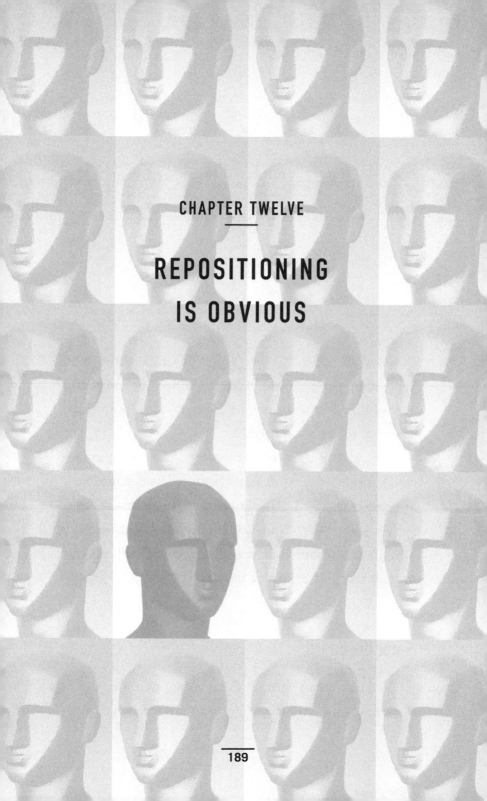

CHAPTER TWELVE

REPOSITIONING
IS OBVIOUS

When it's time for you to reposition, the problem you face will be obvious, and the solution to the problem will be obvious. But people tend not to see the obvious.

General Motors' need to reposition itself has been obvious for decades, as its market share has declined year by year over a quarter of a century. To dramatize this, here's what I wrote in 2001 in a book entitled *Big Brands. Big Trouble.* It wasn't a prediction that came true. It was an obvious observation.

Enter the Board

With the declining market share, it's not surprising that some years ago the board revolted and ejected top management. In recent years, we've seen new CEOs that weren't bean counters, a new marketing chief, brand managers: You name it and it's been tried. But nothing so far has seemed to drive that market share uphill.

The latest effort is the youngest CEO ever appointed. At 47, Rick Wagoner plans to dislodge the insular management style and to bring GM up to Internet speed with e-everything. Will this "Digital Drive" be enough? Will people want to buy GM cars because they are rolling communications devices that are connected to the Internet? Or because they have an "On Star" button on the dashboard? (Hey, Batman has one on his Bat Car.) Will a digital supply chain help GM make cars faster, cheaper, and more customized? Maybe it will. But GM's last fling with technology à la robotics didn't change things very much. And this brave new digital technology doesn't address the basic problem.

General Motors has forgotten what made them successful. It all comes down to the same situation that Sloan faced over 80 years ago. How could GM sort out and position their several brands so they would be different and work together on a complementary basis? The answer took major surgery in 1921 as Sloan exited two brands, consolidated activities, and repositioned what was left. Fixing things in 2001 will probably take major surgery again. Phasing Oldsmobile out is a good start but it won't be easy dealing with old customers, union complaints, and dealer problems.

Well, Wagoner is gone, as are Pontiac, Saturn, Opal, Saab, and the Hummer. We now know just how bad all this was for business. But it took a financial crisis and bankruptcy to get management to deal with what has been obvious for years. One could ask the following question.

What's Going on Here?

The same thing is true with many big, obvious problems. Either hope springs eternal or people want to kick the problem down the road for someone else to handle. This is known as the "psychology of avoidance." A psychology professor at the University of Oregon is the author of a book on this phenomenon and how our minds assess risks. Several of his observations are pertinent to the GM situation.

Threats get our attention when they are imminent, while our brain circuitry is often cavalier about the future. This is why people are irrational about saving for retirement. It's why losing a share point or two year after year just didn't prompt sweeping concern at GM. "We'll just make some adjustments, cut some costs, and get it back next year" probably became management's view of things.

The professor goes on to point out that we're far more sensitive to changes that are instantaneous than to those that are gradual. His point is that the human species is far more programmed to deal with predators and enemies in the Pleistocene Age than with twenty-first-century challenges. The financial crisis was indeed instantaneous.

Piers Steel, an assistant professor in human resources and organizational dynamics at Canada's University of Calgary, also has some insights about procrastination. His feeling is that the reason we procrastinate may be more about confidence than about perfectionism.

"Essentially, procrastinators have less confidence in themselves, less expectancy that they can actually complete a task," Steel said in a University of Calgary news release. "Perfectionism is not the culprit," he continued. "In fact, perfectionists procrastinate less, but they worry about it more."

Steel reviewed procrastination research from scholarly books, conferences, journals, and other sources. His analysis appeared in the January 2007 edition of the American Psychological Association's *Psychological Bulletin*. Procrastination has been around ever since civilization began and "does not appear to be disappearing anytime soon," wrote Steel.

Facing Reality

The antidote for the way we are wired against risk is a heavy dose of reality from an outside observer and a willingness to have an open mind. The biggest problem you'll face is a decision in which people are already invested. This brings to mind a meeting we had with a large company that was about to embark on what we considered an ill-conceived multimillion-dollar assortment of new products. After a presentation on why this line of products was likely to fail, the vice chairman appeared to be convinced that we were right. He looked at us and said, "Where were you a year ago, when we presented all this to the board?"

While the problems were obvious, the launch of these products went forward. There was too much ego invested. By the way, as predicted, the products all failed. It cost the company a fortune, but it gave me a great story to tell.

Let's move on to obvious solutions that also are often hard to sell.

Consultants Sell Complexity

Obvious ideas or solutions often suffer from being too simple. People say, "We know that." They often feel that answers require a high degree of sophistication and complexity. And business consultants only reinforce these perceptions.

In the beginning there was Peter Drucker, quietly dishing out sound management advice. As Andy Grove, the former Intel CEO, put it, "Drucker is a hero of mine. He writes and thinks with exquisite clarity—a standout among a bunch of muddled fad mongers."*

Then in the 1980s, Tom Peters exploded on the scene with his book about excellence. That was the dawning of an era of Tom Peters wannabes whom one could safely call modern-day Robin Hoods. They rob from the rich and keep it. But instead of bows and arrows, this crowd is armed with complex buzzwords and ideas that it uses to nail its prey.

An article in *Fortune* magazine entitled "In Search of Suckers" put it quite accurately: "Quietly, without fanfare, the advice business has been hijacked. New gurus armed with nothing more than pens, podiums and tremendous shamelessness have co-opted what used to be a nice, wholesome calling: dishing out good advice to business men and women."†

Rupert Murdoch was a little more blunt when he was asked whether there was any management guru that he

---

* Bob Lenzner, "Still the Youngest Mind," *Forbes*, March 10, 1997.
† Alan Farnham, "In Search of Suckers," *Fortune*, October 14, 1996, p. 119.

followed or admired. His response: "Guru? You find a gem here or there. But most of it's fairly obvious, you know. You go to the bookstore business section and you see all these wonderful titles and you spend $300 and then you throw them all away."[*]

Even Tom Peters admits, "We're the only society that believes it can keep getting better and better. So we keep on getting suckered in by people like me."[†]

The High Cost of Complexity

Much has been written about the good, the bad, and the ugly of the consulting business. Many consultants, it appears, believe that companies won't pay a lot for simplicity. In fact, it may be that the less a company understands about the process, the more it will pay.

If the solution were simple, companies would do it themselves.

So the trick is to constantly invent new complex concepts. For example, most companies can understand competing in the marketplace. So in an article in the *McKinsey Quarterly* magazine,[‡] readers are told that there are now two worlds in which they have to com-

---

[*] John Micklethwait and Adrian Wooldridge, *The Witch Doctors* (New York: Times Books, 1996).

[†] Farnham, "In Search of Suckers."

[‡] Jeffrey F. Rayport and John J. Sviokla, "Competing in Two Worlds," *McKinsey Quarterly*, January 1996.

---

pete: the marketplace and a new one called the "marketspace." (Nice; it even rhymes.) All this is about creating digital assets, a concept that causes the eyes of a 60-year-old CEO to begin to glaze over.

Then, to introduce a little terror into the equation, the reader is warned that "old business axioms no longer apply" and that companies "must oversee a physical value chain, but must also build and exploit a virtual value chain."

What the authors are hoping for is the following reader response: "Quick, get me the phone number of those two Harvard guys who wrote the article I don't understand. We could be in trouble."

We're not saying that all this information is bad, but it's tough enough for the CEO to figure out how to survive in the marketplace, let alone in a new thing called the marketspace.

In Search of the Obvious

If they are to work, positioning and repositioning ideas must be obvious ideas. That's because they are evident ideas. And if they are evident to you, they will also be evident to your customers, which is why they will work.

In 1916, Robert R. Updegraff wrote a pamphlet entitled *Obvious Adams: The Story of a Successful Busi-*

nessman. It is the best piece on marketing I've ever read. In fact, my last book was on this subject (*In Search of the Obvious*).

Updegraff warned of how obvious ideas are hard to sell when he wrote, "The trouble is, the obvious is apt to be so simple and commonplace that it has no appeal to the imagination. We all like clever ideas and ingenious plans that make good lunch-table talk at the club. There is something about the obvious that is—well, so very obvious?"

Updegraff laid out five tests of obviousness:

1. *This problem, when solved, will be simple.* The obvious is nearly always simple—so simple that sometimes a whole generation of men and women have looked at it without even seeing it. In fact, if an idea is clever, ingenious, or complicated, we should suspect it. It probably is not obvious.

2. *Does it check with human nature?* The obvious matches existing perceptions. People see it in its simple reality, uncomplicated by professional or technical knowledge.

3. *Put it on paper.* Write out your idea, plan, or project in words of one or two syllables, as though you were explaining it to a child. Can you do this in two or three short paragraphs, so that it makes

sense? If not—if the explanation becomes long, involved, or ingenious—then very likely it is not obvious. For, to repeat, "When you find the answer, it will be simple."

4. *Does it explode in people's minds?* If, when you have presented your idea, outlined your solution to a problem, or explained your plan, project, or program, people say, "Now why didn't we think of that before?" you can feel encouraged. For obvious ideas are very apt to produce this "explosive" mental reaction.

5. *Is the time ripe?* Many ideas and plans are obvious in themselves, but just as obviously "out of time." Checking the timeliness is often just as important as checking the idea or plan itself. A repositioning that's ahead of its time or after its time is a big problem.

An Obvious Hospital Repositioning

The answer was both simple and obvious when we were called in a few years ago to work with Orange Regional Medical Center in lower New York State.

Today, Orange Regional is nationally recognized as a Thomson Reuters "Top 100" hospital. But back then, research showed that it was underappreciated for the caliber of its physicians and the sophistication of its technology.

It needed help in shaking off a "nice little community hospital" perception to compete with dozens of hospitals in its region.

The obvious repositioning came from its own vision statement, which was widely circulated but underappreciated: "To create a true regional healthcare enterprise that provides the highest level and broadest possible range of services that are sustainable in the community."

"Is that true?" we asked. The broadest possible range of services? Indeed it was. (A spreadsheet tally of Orange Regional's services vs. competitors' services proved the point that Orange Regional offered more.)

"No One Does More for Your Health" was the repositioning that brought that idea to life. It differentiated the hospital. It gave consumers a simple, strong reason to choose it. It set a standard for how the hospital should continue to perform.

This repositioning exploded in the minds of physicians, trustees, employees, and the community. Five years later, it continued to resonate with them. We think Mr. Updegraff would have approved.

To give you a sense of just how obvious repositioning strategies are, let's visit some random marketing situations with some observations about what should be done.

New Zealand Tourism

In the game of repositioning, beware of meaningless slogans. New Zealand's latest slogan promotes this country as "the youngest country on earth." Now there's a silly idea when you consider that people want to see the old, not the new. What's painfully obvious is the physical beauty of this country. Since New Zealand has two islands, the way to dramatize this is to raise the question of which island is the most beautiful. The repositioning answer: "New Zealand. The world's two most beautiful islands."

If you ask anyone who has visited New Zealand about her view of the country, chances are you'll hear, "It's beautiful." Nothing could be more obvious.

Sri Lanka Tourism

While we are writing about countries, what do you do when you have a negative reputation? Sri Lanka, with its highly publicized civil war, has what we call a badly damaged brand name. It's an anchor to the country's moving forward. This looks like a case for repositioning. Our recommendation would be to go back to the country's original name: Ceylon. This conjures up its romantic past. It is where the tea is grown. It's analogous to Leningrad going back to St. Petersburg.

This is an obvious idea that would be difficult to sell, as there is a lot of country ego in play. But it is how the country should be repositioned.

McDonald's

You've all seen the slogans about "I'm lovin' it." That doesn't strike me as much of a differentiating idea. When you read McDonald's billboard about billions of hamburgers served or when you see its global reach even into places where it doesn't sell hamburgers (like India), the obvious repositioning idea emerges: "McDonald's. The world's favorite place to eat."

Leadership is a very powerful competitive strategy because, as you saw in the introduction, psychologists will tell you that people buy what others buy.

Sears

Once upon a time Sears was the king of retailing as well as catalog buying. Today, the catalog is gone, and the big-box stores are threatening to take away retailing as well. It sounds like a case of reposition or die.

Well, the one thing Sears still has is its big brands, such as Craftsman tools, Kenmore appliances, DieHard batteries, Lands' End clothing, and others in tires and paint. Many of these brands are leaders in their respective categories.

With these in the stores, the obvious repositioning strategy should be, "Home of America's best brands." And Sears's marketing should be more about these brands and less about the stores, beyond saying that these brands can be found only at Sears.

So what's happening? There is discussion about selling these brands in other retail outlets. That could be the end of Sears as a retailer.

Newsweek

Newsweek and its competitor *Time* magazine have lost a great deal of their circulation and a lot of advertising. Both are trying to avoid the fate of *US News & World Report*, once a weekly, now a monthly, and barely hanging on. While they are fading, *The Economist* is thriving. It looks like a job for repositioning.

First, *Newsweek* must realize that it is no *Economist,* with its globe-saturating coverage. It must also realize that general interest is out and niche is in. The problem is what niche to preempt. If you were running *Newsweek,* the first thing you should realize is that a redesign does not change anything. It's like rearranging the deck chairs on the *Titanic.* What is called for is a new idea, not a new design.

The obvious repositioning idea would be to focus on brand-name columnists, not the news. People like George Will, Fareed Zakaria, Robert Samuelson, and

Jonathan Alter are reasons to buy the magazine. Brand-name columnists create a point of difference. They give you a valuable perspective on the news and what it all means. I would even add an overview entitled "The Blogosphere," where someone would cover the good, the bad, and the ugly that's online.

Another new column idea would be one by Jon Stewart of *Daily Show* fame. Jon could cover the ridiculous, of which there are many examples. He would also be a big draw for younger readers.

The only problem with this repositioning is the name, *Newsweek*. This magazine isn't about news. It's more about opinions than about news. It should be called *Opinion Week,* and it should reposition itself as offering "insights about the news."

The main reason for this bold and different move is that repositioning your brand today is so much harder than it was in the old days—especially when you're destined to be seen as a copycat product. And its number one competitor, *Time,* has also been through a redesign.

This case study clearly illustrates what repositioning is all about. It adjusts perceptions closer to what *Newsweek* has become. It's a strong competitive move in a time of crisis. It requires some courage to make the change. It's all very obvious, and it will take some money and time to accomplish.

Throughout the book, we've written about other obvious repositioning strategies, such as Chevrolet being "America's favorite American car" or Continental Airlines offering "More airline for the money." None of these are very clever. These are just obvious repositioning ideas to be used in a time of competition, change, and crisis.

Throughout the decades that I've been writing and speaking about this subject, I've tried to keep my work simple and obvious as a way to demonstrate how people should do their marketing.

Meanwhile, the so-called experts in the field have worked hard at trying to keep things complicated and confusing.

My final advice is, try not to overresearch or overthink your positioning or repositioning strategy. Simple and obvious will do the trick.

EPILOGUE

In a way, this book ends a journey that started in 1969 when I wrote the first article on positioning, entitled "Positioning Is a Game People Play in Today's Me-Too Marketplace."

Since that time, "positioning" and "repositioning" have become heavily used words in business all around the globe. If you have any doubt, do a word search online; you'll find that those two words appear millions of times. In business publications around the world, the two words appeared 37,163 times during 2008.

And yet to this day, while many people use the word *positioning,* not all of them truly understand what it is all about. And influential groups such as management consultants have little idea about perceptions or winning or losing in the mind.

So now both positioning and repositioning have been presented in detail. In between, I have written 14 other books about various aspects of this subject.

If people don't get it now, they never will. And in this highly competitive world, that only means big trouble for them.

All I can say is that I warned you, and, as Edward R. Murrow used to say, "Good night and good luck."

INDEX

INDEX

INDEX

INDEX

INDEX

INDEX

ABOUT THE AUTHORS

Jack Trout

Jack Trout, legendary marketing strategist, is the acclaimed author of many marketing classics published in many languages: *Positioning: The Battle for Your Mind*, *Marketing Warfare* (updated in the 20th Anniversary edition), *The 22 Immutable Laws of Marketing*, *Differentiate or Die*, *Big Brands: Big Trouble*, *A Genie's Wisdom*, and *Trout on Strategy*. Following the second edition of *Differentiate or Die*, he most recently published *In Search of the Obvious: The Antidote for Today's Marketing Mess*.

President of Trout & Partners Ltd. an international marketing consultancy based in Connecticut, Jack Trout has consulted for many companies, including Hewlett-Packard, Southwest Airlines, Merck, Procter & Gamble, and Papa John's Pizza. He has consulted with the State Department on how to better sell America, and in 2006 he helped the Democrats regain leadership of the U.S. Congress.

Recognized as one of the world's foremost marketing strategists, Trout is the originator of Positioning and other important concepts in marketing strategy. He has more than 40 years of experience in advertising and marketing, and became a boardroom advisor to some of the world's largest corporations. His worldwide consulting work gives him first-hand experience in a wide range of marketing scenarios. Jack Trout has gained an international reputation as a consultant, writer, speaker, and proponent of leading-edge marketing strategies.

Steve Rivkin

Steve Rivkin, a naming expert and long-time partner with Trout & Partners, has previously coauthored three books with Jack Trout: *The New Positioning*, *The Power of Simplicity*, and *Differentiate or Die*.

Steve founded Rivkin & Associates LLC, a marketing and communications consultancy, in 1989, in Glen Rock, N.J. His firm has consulted for such clients as Alstom, Baptist Health System, IdeaVillage, Kraft Foods, PixelOptics, Premio Foods, and Thomson Healthcare. Steve has coauthored two other books: *IdeaWise*, a guide to borrowing and adapting new ideas; and *The Making of a Name*, on the strategic, creative, linguistic, and legal aspects of brand names.

He is a frequent speaker on marketing and communications topics, and has appeared at hundreds of conferences and seminars in the United States, Europe, and Southeast Asia.

Visit Steve's Web site at www.Rivkin.net.